In the Grip of the Past:

Educational Reforms that Address What should Be Changed and What Should be Conserved

By

C. A. Bowers

Eco-Justice Press, LLC
Eugene, Oregon, USA

Printed in the United States of America

Eco-Justice Press, L.L.C.
P.O. Box 5409 Eugene, OR 97405
www.ecojusticepress.com

Text and cover design: David Diethelm

Cover photos:
"Environmental Eyesore" ©iStockphoto.com/kozmoat98
"Potter's Hands" ©iStockphoto.com/ntarres
"Craftsman in Turkey..." ©iStockphoto.com/ozenli
"Vegetable Garden" ©iStockphoto.com/aluxum

Library of Congress Control Number: 2013934696
ISBN 978-0-9891296-1-9

In the Grip of the Past:
Educational Reforms that Address What should
Be Changed and What Should be Conserved
By C.A. Bowers

Also by C. A. Bowers

The Promise of Theory: Education and the Politics of Cultural Change

Elements of a Post-Liberal Theory of Education

The Cultural Dimensions of Educational Computing: Understanding the Non-Neutrality of Technology

(with David Flinders) Responsive Teaching: An Ecological Approach to Classroom Patterns of Language, Culture, and Thought

Education, Cultural Myths, and the Ecological Crisis: Toward Deep Changes

Critical Essays on Education, Modernity, and the Recovery of the Ecological Imperative

Educating for an Ecologically Sustainable Culture: Re-thinking Moral Education, Creativity, Intelligence, and Other Modern Orthodoxies

The Culture of Denial: Why the Environmental Movement Needs a Strategy for Reforming Universities and Public Schools

Let Them Eat Data: How Computers Affect Education, Cultural Diversity, and Prospects of Ecological Sustainability

Educating for Eco-Justice and Community

Detras de la Apariencia: Hacia la descolonizacion de la Educacion

Mindful Conservatism: Rethinking the Ideological and Educational basis of of an Ecologically Sustainable Future

Rethinking Freire: Globalization and the Environmental Crisis (co-edited with Frederique Apffel-Marglin)

The False Promises of Constructivist Theories of Learning

Revitalizing the Commons: Cultural and Educational Sites of Resistance and Affirmation

Perspectives on the Ideas of Gregory Bateson, Ecological Intelligence, and Educational Reforms

University Reform in an Era of Global Warming

Educational Reforms for the 21st Century

The Way Forward:Educational Reforms that Focus on the Cultural Common and the Linguistic Roots of the Ecologial/Cultural Crises

How to Lose a Democracy

First, believe you can have
whatever you want
whenever you want it.

Make the desire concrete—
white goods or appliances or jewelry—
anything you can't afford.

And let someone else define it,
so that what you do not need
you cannot do without.

Forget the night sky
and clear water over rocks after rain.
Forget to say what you see,
and courage, forget courage entirely.

Cede what you know to be right
to comfort and plenty. Ask the land
to bear each wound. Ask the animals
to leave their nests and lairs.

Having lost so much, it will be easy
to unhinge language,
to unname each flower and tree.

You see how little it will take
to fail at what you say you believe.

History will say you lost your nerve,
if anyone has the nerve to write history.

Kathryn Kirkpatrick, *Our Held Animal Breath* (2012)

Contents

Chapter 1

Introduction:

The title of this collection of essays, *In the Grip of the Past*, was deliberately chosen as it highlights what both market liberals (misnamed conservatives) and the progressive/emancipatory educational reformers totally misunderstand. Both promote progress and a lifestyle of continual change; with technological innovations that drive new markets being the goal of market liberals, and with transformative learning and individual freedom being the goal of the progressive/emancipatory educational reformers. Both groups draw their inspiration from abstract theorists who were, in turn, dependent upon earlier abstract and ethnocentric theories that can be traced back to John Locke and Adam Smith and for the educational reformers, the ethnocentric and Social Darwinian theories of John Dewey, Paulo Freire, Moacir Gadotti, and their many eco-pedagogy followers. Both groups also experienced the advances in technology, the spread of western values and ways of thinking, and what genuinely appeared as progress in raising people's material standard of living. But their perceptions were limited by a lack of awareness of how progress in the sciences and technology involved introducing toxins that have altered the prospects of all life renewing processes, as well as how promoting the industrial/consumer-dependent culture as the model for the future is quickly exceeding the life-sustaining capacity of natural systems.

Perhaps even more important is the failure of market liberals and progress-oriented educational reformers to understand that the DNA of all living things influences how the past continues to influence the present and future. The past is not something that we can move away from because our patterns of thinking have been influenced by what Edward Shils refers to as the "anti-tradition tradition" encoded in our language and mythopoetic narratives of what it means to be modern and living according to the prescriptions of the western Enlightenment. Without an awareness of the many ways we continue to be in the grip of the past, proposals for reform will be characterized by double bind thinking. That is, the solutions will not be based on an adequate understanding of local problems and possibilities.

Recent changes in both the cultural and natural ecologies, which now represent decline rather than progress, could not be anticipated given the ideologies promoted in public schools and universities. Yet, today's advocates of market liberalism (and libertarianism) and the emancipation-oriented educational reformers continue to promote changes that foster a sense of ecological and cultural rootlessness. Today's scientists, market liberals, and the social justice educational reformers continue to assume they can overcome in their different ways any setback in the Darwinian march into a better future. They also continue to promote the silences that replicate the hubris of the Titanic mindset that was unaware of the dangers that lie ahead. One of these most important silences relates to knowing what needs to be intergenerationally renewed in this era of rapid deterioration in natural systems, in the viability of the democratic process, and in the global spread of market liberalism that is undermining such basics as food security and other life-supporting systems.

One of the ironies is that while progress (also known as "development," "modernization," "globalization") is still widely understood as overcoming the hold of the past, many of the earlier achievements within the world's diverse cultures are still part of daily life in many communities. What has gone unnoticed by the progress-oriented reformers and policy makers is that these traditions have a smaller ecological impact. Many have also served as the basis of mutual support systems that represented local alternatives to the money-driven market system. In thinking about these earlier achievements that are becoming increasingly relevant in today's ecologically-stressed world, it is necessary to avoid the non-reflective rejection of the past, which is the Achilles heel of the promoters of progress.

The past has indeed left a legacy of human injustices that are still promoted by powerful forces that exist in different cultures. And this legacy carries forward many of the ways of thinking and values that are at the root of the cultural and ecological crises. One of the achievements of the progressive/emancipatory educational reformers is that they have focused attention on that part of the legacy that still promotes race, class, and gender discrimination. But like the market liberals who consider all traditions (which is another way of referring to what is being carried forward from the past) as obstacles to turning every aspect of daily life into market opportunities, the progressive/emancipatory educational reformers also consider all traditions as sources of oppression and limitations on the fullest expression of individual freedom. Indeed, their concept of emancipation and their association of critical inquiry with a linear form of progress are seldom qualified in ways that suggest they are aware that not all of the legacy from the past should be overturned. Nor do their writings suggest that questions about which traditions that should be carried forward should be decided within each culture—and not by ethnocentric western educators who are particularly lacking in a deep knowledge of the traditions of other cultures. It must be added that few of these educational reformers have a deep knowledge of the traditions of their own culture; thus their silence about how being embedded in the grip of the past continue to be sources of empowerment.

Their silences are replicated by the market liberals (including the scientists and digital technologists) who promote change without giving careful consideration to how their innovations lead to the loss of intergenerational knowledge, skills, and achievements—particularly in the area of civil liberties. Privacy is now gone, and many of our civil liberties are also under threat from corporations and their extremist allies. The legacy from the past that enabled people to be more self sufficient in the areas of producing and sharing food, healing, creative arts, craft knowledge, narratives, mutual support systems, and, most importantly, knowledge of the life cycles of plants and animals in their bioregion, is also now being replaced by increasing reliance upon the industrial system of production and consumption and the cultural amnesia that results from the increased reliance upon the Internet. Economic and ideologically-driven globalization are also contributing to the loss of local traditions that were the basis, in many cultures, of the mutual support systems that represented the many forms of non-monetized wealth found in the cultural and environmental commons.

The abstract words in the above sentences reflect the same limitations as the words of the market liberals and the scientists and technologists who are complicit in overturning the genuine achievements that are part of the legacy of the past. My reliance upon the use of words (that is, iconic metaphors) also reflects the limitations found in the writings of Dewey, Freire, and Gadotti. The printed word inherently reproduces an abstract and thus limited representation of the sensory, context-dependent, and culturally and linguistically layered world that people experience largely at a taken for granted level of awareness.

It is the taken for granted status of these cultural patterns that leads people to ignore how the printed word differs from the spoken word. Print, in spite of its widespread use and constant updating, is unable to represent the dynamic interactions between the participants in the micro and macro cultural and natural ecologies. These ecologies need to be understood as ecologies of signs, which can also be understood as interactive webs of communication. Whether these signs are recognized, and how they elicit a response from the Other depends upon whether the organism processes the information at the chemical, genetic, sensory level, or as in the case of humans at the more complex level of all of the above plus reliance on a metaphorical language that both hides and illuminates what is being communicated in the ever changing relationships.

Deep ethnographically informed written accounts of people's beliefs and daily practices have been written. Some even provide insightful accounts of cultural legacies of ecological wisdom of how to live in supportive relationships with each other and within the limits and possibilities of the natural systems they depend upon. But these accounts, as well as the legacy of ecological wisdom handed down in many of the daily practices of the cultural commons, largely go unrecognized. The legacy of print-based abstract thinking has its roots in the dominant meta-narratives of mainstream culture, in the ethnocentric theories of economic and political philosophers, and in the years of being conditioned to associate the printed word with high-status knowledge. Internet mediated thinking and communication, now leaves even the average person alienated from what could be learned from the ecologies of communication (signs) within the natural and cultural worlds. The droughts and other extreme manifestations of weather, as well as the devastated habitats that foul rivers with toxins that also disrupt the immune and other systems in the human body, should alert everyone relying upon their five senses, plus memory of how far the deterioration has progressed in their lifetime, to consider how abstract thinking and print-based representations undermine awareness of the relationships and interdependencies that connect individual lives to the larger ecosystems now being threatened.

This is one of the ironies of the modern era. Print and other systems of abstract representation have led to huge benefits in humankind's march from its watery beginnings. Now, however, the genuine achievements of the past are in danger of being lost as digitally-based surveillance becomes more widespread, as computer-driven automation eliminates human skills and even the need for workers, as wealth increasingly flows into the hands of the already super-rich who now work to subvert our democratic traditions, and as the hard core market liberals and other extremists view environmentalists as the new terrorists. These environmentally and community destructive ways of thinking and practices, which Bateson refers to as ecologies of bad ideas, are rooted in the past that should not be allowed to continue. And the cultural traditions in the West and elsewhere that represent community-centered alternatives to the modern industrial/consumer-dependent lifestyle should be intergenerationally renewed.

This collection of essays addresses the more critically important educational reform issues of the day. Perhaps the most important is the need for the proponents of the UNESCO sponsored 10 year agenda for transforming teacher education to consider the danger of basing reforms on western ideas that were uninformed about the cultural roots of the ecological crisis. What is important about this global effort to promote reforms in teacher education is that it is supposed to promote ecologically sustainable development within different cultures. The problem is that the western educational reformers, who are providing the conceptual direction for this global effort, are unaware that the ideas they are promoting are derived from western ethnocentric and Social Darwinian thinkers. This is, in itself, a serious problem. But there is the added problem that Dewey, Freire, Gadotti, and their current proponents failed to recognize that the ecological crisis now requires a shift in the basic paradigm now guiding the globalization of the digital phase of the industrial revolution. The challenge today is not how to introduce technologies that will further foster people's dependence upon labor saving machines (which will lead to more unemployment), provide for seamless surveillance of people's activities (which provides the infrastructure for a police state and more corporate intrusion into people's lives), and greater computer-mediated and thus print-based thinking (which fosters both cultural amnesia and abstract thinking that undermines the exercise of ecological intelligence). Rather, the shift in thinking needs to abandon the Enlightenment misconceptions about traditions so that a more balanced approach can lead to recognizing what needs to be conserved within the diverse cultural commons of the world, and what needs to be reformed. The irony is that the modernizing ideology that is overshooting the sustaining capacity of natural systems and is the driving force in colonizing other cultures to adopt an ecologically unsustainable lifestyle is also part of the legacy of the past. The challenge is to identify which legacy inherited from the past will enable a world population now moving toward the 10 billion mark to meet the basic essentials for sustaining a meaningful life.

There is also an essay that challenges two dominant patterns in teacher education courses: one being the survey course that leaves future teachers without a depth of understanding of the educational reforms they are asked to consider. The other is the tendency of the professor to ride her/his own horse rather than address how to engage students in learning about the ecologically sustainable and unsustainable traditions and patterns within their own culture they are likely to take for granted.

This essay explains how the process of naming the cultural patterns—such as how the metaphorical language carries forward the misconceptions and insights from the past, how the cultural commons are being enclosed by market forces, and how print and computer-mediated learning undermine the exercise of ecological intelligence—engages students in learning about the tacit patterns within their own culture. This deep ethnography approach to learning, which can begin in the early grades and sustained through to graduate level courses, avoids the limitations of reading abstract (print-based) accounts of other cultures that may be of little interest to students. What students most need in this era of political and ecological uncertainties is to understand their own cultural patterns and relationships, particularly the relationships that are mutually supportive as well as those that are destructive. The role of the classroom teacher and professor is to name, and thus to bring to explicit awareness, the patterns and relationships that need to be examined—again from the perspective of what is community enhancing and ecologically sustainable. Learning to give close attention to how the students' ideas and behaviors affect their relationships with others, including the natural environmental, is also important to learning how to exercise ecological intelligence.

The third essay in this collection examines what is being claimed as the next revolution in higher education, which will be the possibility of obtaining an online degree from the higher status universities and colleges. The important issues considered in this essay include how online degrees, which rely upon print and thus abstract knowledge and communication, hide the linguistic colonization that occurs when words are mistakenly assumed to refer to real entities and events, and not recognized as metaphors framed by the assumptions and analogs settled upon in the distant past—and within a specific culture. With the development of the technology that enables tests to be machine scored universities will be able to vastly increase their revenues while reducing the need for faculty (much in the same way the Internet has reduced staffs of newspapers). Another consequence of online degrees is that future employers will be able to access information about what students may have read in their courses, which will allow employers to judge the student's political correctness. Online courses taken by thousands of students from around the world also contributes to increasing the influence of the narrowed interpretative framework of the professor who creates the course that is then copyrighted by the university. This shift from face to face communication in the classroom, and in other learning environments where students encounter a variety of interpretations, to print-based and other media presentations that are largely taken out of context is also a key issue being overlooked in the rush to offer the less expensive online degrees that will attract more students who are facing the increasingly uncertainty of being able to find work in their chosen field.

The essay on the thinking of Ayn Rand is another example of how our political discourse continues in the grip of the past. Her widespread influence on market liberals who now are in control of the Supreme Court, the legislative branch of Congress, as well as in many state governments, is not surprising when her place in the history of western philosophy is considered. What is distinctive about the mainstream thinking among western philosophers is that they relied upon print and thus abstract thinking as their primary mode of communication. They also were ethnocentric thinkers, and they totally ignored the traditions of cultural knowledge, skills, and patterns of mutual support that sustained the cultural commons and thus the life of the community on a largely non-monetized basis.

It is to be expected that Ayn Rand's explanation of the virtue of selfishness, and the supposedly universal prescriptions of how a capitalist economy will reward those who pursue their own interests, would not be challenged by people who have undergone years of learning to think in terms of abstract theory. The role of local markets in different cultural contexts, as well as the different cultural patterns that govern reciprocity and patterns of mutual support, are simply not considered by Rand. Just as her key metaphors reproduce the ethnocentric thinking of most western philosophers, her followers fail to recognize that they too are guilty of relying upon context-free metaphors for which there is no criteria for using language in an accountable manner. As abstractions, the language is assumed to represent what is universal about the core features of the human condition, and there is no way to challenge them— especially as her universal pronouncements align with other abstract theories such as Social Darwinism and historically derived theories about the self-correcting mechanisms of free markets. The historical pathway of abstract theory upon which she relies will replicate other recent disasters such as the reliance of the German Nazis on the theory of Social Darwinism. Both lead to mythic thinking that is especially problematic in today's era of ecological collapse.

The recent mega-droughts and storms such as Sandy are the real test of the relevance of her abstract pronouncements on how life should be lived, and what responsibilities people have toward each other. As pointed out in the essay, Rand's ideas are totally divorced from understanding either her own adopted culture or what is ecologically distinctive about other cultures. As the ecological crisis deepens, and civil unrest reaches a crisis point, people conditioned to think in abstractions will be willing to follow other demagogues—which again will demonstrate that supposedly highly educated people are still in the grip of one of the worst traditions handed down from the past: that is, the herd instinct that demagogues rely upon. The important question raised by the widespread influence that Rand's ideas have had on today's political process should focus on how public schools and universities have failed. This is the same question that needed to be asked about the failure of formal education in Nazi Germany.

How the leaders of the Occupy Movement failed to recognize the importance of the cultural commons provides another example of how the thinking of different reform efforts are still in the grip of the past. But the past that the leaders of the Occupy Movement could not escape is the silence that has resulted from what public schools and universities have regarded as high-status and thus as worthy of being included in the curriculum. The low-status knowledge, which is largely excluded from what is learned in publics schools, universities, and from the mind-shaping media, is what exists in every community. It is the intergenerational knowledge, skills, and mentoring relationships that are largely shared outside of a money economy. As the intergenerational knowledge and skills vary from culture to culture, it should be called the 'cultural commons." Given the unemployment, poverty, and wasted lives that the Occupy Movement was addressing, the revitalization of the local cultural commons should have been part of the strategy for moving the protests from the streets to learning how to participate in the local cultural commons. In addition to learning how to live less money-dependent lives, the cultural commons support community-centered lifestyles that have a smaller toxic and carbon footprint.

In short, learning how to participate in the gift economy where wealth is shared in the forms of knowledge and skills handed down over generations in preparing food, learning healing practices, discovering talents in the creative arts, learning a craft, carrying forward traditions that support civil liberties—as well as all the other ethnically diverse activities that reduce dependency upon consumerism and thus the money economy—should become part of the strategy of the post-Occupy Movement leaders. As work becomes increasingly taken over by computer driven machines, and as the quest for even greater profits excludes more people from full or even partial employment (and thus from participating in the money economy), learning the traditions still carried on in different cultures that represent alternatives to the consumer-dependent lifestyle required by the Industrial Revolution represents one of the more positive aspects of being in the grip of the past. But even this legacy must be examined critically, as the cultural commons of many communities still carry forward unjust and morally problematic practices.

Concern about the traditions that are being undermined by computer-driven technologies is the focus of the chapter that addresses the current efforts to introduce computer-based learning in cultures that still rely upon orality as a primary form of cultural storage and thinking. The loss of traditions of craft knowledge and skills, of community solidarity and mutual support, of face-to-face relationships that are the basis of mentoring, of the multiple forms of information accessed by the senses and stored as memories of life-enhancing ecologies, of other cultural ways of knowing and sensory-based experiences, and of the possibility of moving to the fullest exercise of ecological intelligence—raises the question of whether the introduction of computers into non-western classrooms yet another example of western colonization. As I have explained elsewhere, print is inherently ethnocentric in that it undermines the oral traditions of communication and cultural storage of cultures whose survival has depended upon the development of ecological intelligence.

Computers, as I argue in this essay, not only undermine the non-monetized wealth that is shared in the local cultural commons, but also the ecological wisdom many oral cultures have achieved through careful observation of living systems. Computer-mediated thinking and storage can make available massive amounts of data relating to changes in the earth's ecosystems. But it cannot communicate wisdom about what contributes to an ecologically sustainable lifestyle. This is because the models of ecosystem behaviors and the data, while important, are always subject to individual and thus ideologically-driven interpretations—which too often becomes a matter of relying upon taken for granted patterns of thinking inherited from earlier thinkers who argued for the primacy of individual thought while ignoring how all forms of life, including that of the individual, are part of the interdependent world of cultural and natural ecologies.

Thus, the focus of this essay is on the cultural colonization that is occurring as non-western students rely more upon computer-mediated learning. The argument is not framed in terms of either-or-categories, but in terms of suggesting the possible cultural gains and losses. There is now a growing awareness that digital technologies are not culturally neutral, and that they are altering consciousness itself. Thus, the discussion of how the educational uses of computers in non-western cultures, especially in cultures whose oral traditions carried forward the ecological intelligence of earlier generations, expands on the emerging discussion of what is being lost that is vital to our collective future survival. This line of inquiry brings into question the tradition inherited from that past that holds that science and technology are culturally neutral, and that questions do not need to be asked about the importance of what is being lost as we follow the scientists and technologists into their version of a progressive future. That the view of progress of many scientists and technologists includes the further genetic engineering of plants and animals, of creating digital technologies that will further bring people's lives under constant surveillance by government and corporations, and of replacing humans in the workplace with computer-driven machines, suggests that the education of scientists (including computer scientists) needs to be radically reformed. Unfortunately, this reform is not likely to happen for the simple reason that few scientists possess the conceptual background for recognizing how their thinking has been framed by the metaphorical language that carries forward the misconceptions and silences from the past—including a way of thinking that fails to consider the traditions being overturned by the constant quest for new innovations and markets.

The last essay returns to yet another issue that is being debated among educational reformers—at least by those who are just beginning to recognize that the curriculum may be related to the environmental disruptions that are affecting people's lives, and to what the environmentalists are trying to bring to the publics attention. That is, this essay explores the differences between social justice-based educational reform efforts, and how the principals of eco-justice provide for a more ecologically coherent conceptual, moral, and classroom practice that addresses what is now the dominant challenge of the 21st century—which is how a population moving toward 10 billion people is going to survive in an environment rapidly being degraded by the excess demands of the industrial/consumer-dependent culture now being globalized. The main argument is that most advocates of social justice-based educational reforms, while addressing important issues, are caught in double bind thinking. While addressing the deep cultural roots of various forms of oppression and marginalization, the future envisioned for these emancipated groups fails to give more than lip-service to the importance of the fundamental changes now taking place as we enter the digital phase of industrial production. The rapid decline in the viability of natural systems that support life is also being ignored.

As this essay points out, in this era of increasing unemployment and mega-environmental disruptions such as droughts and extreme storms (as well as the impact of toxins and the changes in the chemistry of the world's oceans), food insecurity and poverty are going to become more widespread. And the newly emancipated social groups will continue to be impacted the greatest. Promoting transformative learning and an expanded sense of individual freedom made sense even in the last decades of the 20th century. But given the new realities of automation and economic globalization, as well as the destructive forces unleashed by the ecological crisis, social justice reforms must now be aligned with one of the main principals of eco-justice thinking: namely, how to introduce the ethnically diverse student populations to the intergenerational knowledge, skills, and mentoring relationships that still exist in their communities. Learning to participate in the cultural commons of these communities, which also requires recognizing those aspects of the local cultural commons that are sources of marginalization and injustice, represents one of the few possibilities for being less dependent upon the money economy that will disappear even further under the impact of a market liberal policies—which even the Democrats embrace. Educational reforms that address social justice issues within the more comprehensive understanding that the ecological crisis will become the dominant challenge in the immediate years ahead will also need to address how to educate students to adopt lifestyles that have a smaller toxic and carbon footprint—and to become communicatively competent in resisting the drive to turn all aspects of daily life into market relationships.

As this essay argues, learning about the culturally diverse cultural commons, and the non-monetized forms of wealth that are shared as students discover talents and develop skills as they participate in their local cultural commons, points to another reason educational reformers need to understand that living in the grip of the past is not always a source of oppression and backwardness. In short, educational reformers focused only on the late 20th century understanding of social justice, and who also framed educational reforms in terms of promoting transformative learning and individual emancipation, need to wake-up to the reality that for centuries different cultures have learned to live in mutually supportive ways, to address issues of food security and the development of the expressive arts, and to foster ecological wisdom of how to live within the limits and possibilities of their local bioregions. That is, these traditions are still carried on in ethnic groups, in rural and urban communities, and within families and mutually supportive social groups. And they involve a different form of learning than what is being promoted by some educational reformers who have made the mantras of "change" and "progress" the keystone for how to prepare students for what lies ahead.

Chapter 2

Is Transformative Learning UNESCO Colonizing Agenda for Global Educational Reforms?

There have been a number of major changes in the world since 1983 when I published the article titled "Linguistic Roots of Cultural Invasion in Paulo Freire's Pedagogy." My critique was prompted by reading the account of two cultural linguists, Ron and Suzanne Wong Scollon. They had studied the differences between the mainstream Western patterns of thinking, and that of the Fort Chipewyan in Northern Alberta. This early effort to clarify the ways in which Freire's ideas, and thus his pedagogy, was based on the assumptions of the western Enlightenment has now been validated by a number of Third World activists who initially were both highly committed and knowledgeable followers of Freire. This group of activist included, among others, Siddhartha (who from 1978-1984 served as the Asian coordinator of Freirean pedagogical methods), Loyda Sanchez (a militant in the Bolivian ELN and worker in the Popular Education movement based on Freirean ideas), Grimaldo Rengifo (co-founder of PRATEC and an early user of Freirean ideas in the Peruvian popular literacy program), and Gustavo Esteva (an activist who works with marginalized indigenous and urban groups in Mexico and Central America). In a collection of essays titled *Rethinking Freire: Globalization and the Environmental Crisis* (Bowers and Apffel-Marglin, 2005), they describe the difficulties they encountered in getting the members of indigenous cultures to engage in the Freirean process of consciousness raising as part of becoming literates and thus becoming abstract thinkers—which was not part of their cultural traditions.

As they explain in their essays, Freire's assumptions about the emancipatory nature of critical reflection, as well as how its practice supposedly leads to the highest expression of humankind's potential, were fundamentally different from the cultural ways of knowing of the indigenous groups with whom these activists worked. What separates the observations of these activists about the western colonizing nature of Freire's pedagogy from the uncritical promoters of his ideas in western colleges of education is that these activists spoke the local languages. Thus, their knowledge of the indigenous cultures they initially set out to transform, and their subsequent realization of how the colonizing influence of Freire's ideas would undermine the local cultural commons, stands in sharp contrast to the ethnocentrism of the promoters of Freire's ideas who have ignored the differences in cultural ways of knowing. Another fundamental difference is that these Third World activists, who are now engaged in cultural affirmation programs that strengthen resistance to economic and technological globalization, are acutely aware of the deepening ecological crisis—which, according to Moacir Gadotti (the Director of the Instituto Paulo Freire in Brazil), Freire only became aware of just before his death.

In addition to the criticisms of these Third World activists, there are other reasons for reassessing the adequacy of the ideas of Freire and John Dewey—and more generally the conceptual foundations of the various interpretations of transformative learning theory. Since publishing my 1983 essay on the colonizing nature of Freire's pedagogy, the rate and scale of environmental changes have become more visible and are now having a greater impact on peoples' lives—from health effects to sinking further into poverty. Unless the environmentally destructive nature of local and global cultural practices are reversed or at least significantly mitigated, conflicts over the control of potable water, fisheries, and sources of energy will become even more widespread. Other changes occurring since 1983 include the acceleration of economic and technologically-based globalization now being driven by a neo-liberal ideology that promotes the outsourcing of work and technologies, efforts to achieve greater efficiencies and profits through further automation that reduces the need for workers, and the reduction in health care and retirement benefits for the workers that remain. This neo-liberal agenda, which is spreading around the world, is being furthered by such international institutions as the World Bank, the World Trade Organizations, and the further merging of western science and the industrial culture. In addition to increasing the rate of environmental degradation, globalization of the West's industrial culture is also undermining the linguistic/cultural diversity that is essential to maintaining biological diversity and to resisting the further spread of a market mentality.

In light of the criticisms of Freire's emancipatory agenda by these Third World activists (Bowers and Apffel-Marglin, 2005), as well as the deepening environmental crisis and the western colonizing trends, it is particularly important to ask the following questions: Why have these environmental changes not led to a critical assessment of the silences, ethnocentrism, misconceptions, and hubris of Freire, Dewey and the many professors of education who promote the spread of transformative learning theories? Why have so many editors of western presses become agents of political correctness by refusing to publish a critical rethinking of the cultural assumptions shared by Freire, Dewey and their many followers? And why is criticism of the promoters of transformative learning theorists rejected on the grounds that it is anti-Marxist (Peter McLaren's claim) and "bashing," as Nicholas Burbules put it, of the ideas of Dewey and Freire? Could it be that the cultural alternatives to economic and technological globalization, and the neo-liberal ideology that globalization is based upon, would require acknowledging that many of the core cultural assumptions that underlie the ideas of Freire, Dewey, and their many followers were also the conceptual underpinnings of the industrial culture?

What is most surprising today is the way the advisors to the UNESCO program are promoting transformative learning as the basis for achieving sustainable development in the world's teacher education programs. Given the diversity of the world's cultures, it is especially noteworthy that the followers of Dewey, Freire, and, now, Moacir Gadotti continue to ignore that all three theorists are both ethnocentric and Social Darwinian thinkers.

The Social Darwinian thinking of the three most important contributors to transformative approaches to education reform, and now to the UNESCO program, should not be viewed as of minor importance. Social Darwinian thinking has been a major contributor to the West's long-term agenda of cultural colonization of the supposedly less-evolved cultures. This continues to be expressed in the current efforts to promote a money economy and dependence on the western patterns of consumerism and technologies that reduce the need for workers. The primary goal of the transformative educational agenda is to lead to autonomous critical thinkers who can promote change. What this Freirean process of self-emancipation is to achieve is to rid the students of their cultural heritage, which includes the intergenerational knowledge of how to live less consumer-dependent and less ecologically disruptive lives.

The irony that has escaped the promoters of the UNESCO agenda of promoting sustainable educational reforms is that critical inquiry does not always lead to progress. What is overlooked by those who adopt the Deweyian and Freirean interpretation of critical inquiry is that it should also enable students to recognize what needs to be conserved that contributes to community self-sufficiency, mutual support, traditions of social justice, and the intergenerational knowledge of how to live within the limits and possibilities of their bioregions. Basing the agenda for global educational reforms in teacher education on transformative theories of learning, which is based on western cultural assumptions, is a classic example of double bind thinking.

The transformative learning theorists who are primarily popularizers of Freire's ideas are critical of capitalism and, now, of economic globalization—but they avoid facing their own complicity in the efforts to globalize the non-economic agenda of western liberalism by referring to the industrial culture as a conservative force. The mislabeling of the ideology and practices of economic globalization as conservative helps to hide the basic reality that is being experienced by nearly everybody on a daily basis: namely, that the growing dominance of a market mentality is forcing people around the world to engage in a form of transformative learning that supports the industrial culture's view of progress. New technologies, innovations that facilitate the globalization of consumer-dependent lifestyles, the constant introduction of new drugs and the accompanying discovery of their health risks, the growing spread of unemployment and underemployment through the ranks of different cultures, and environmental changes ranging from the pollution of water to the decline in fisheries, are forcing transformations in how people think and respond to the increasing rate of change.

Further evidence of transformative learning that does not fit the progressive vision of Dewey, Freire and their followers includes how global warming is changing the basic weather patterns of the Inuit of Northern Canada, which forces them to relearn how to read the new and increasingly unpredictable weather patterns. Extreme weather, ranging from floods to droughts, is also forcing people to engage in yet other forms of transformative learning where the old patterns that sustained everyday life must now be changed. The increasing amount of mercury now found in North American lakes, for examples, also makes it necessary to engage in transformative learning—including where to find fish that has not been contaminated as well as how to deal with the physical deformation of children caused by mercury and other toxins which will become for their parents a lifelong transformative learning experience that also differs from the educational theorist's romantic vision.

These examples, which could be multiplied many times over, are cited in order to make the point that the environmental changes resulting from the industrial/consumer-based cultures are not based on conservative values and guiding ideas found in the writings of Edmund Burke, Vandana Shiva, and Wendell Berryñor in the practices of cultures that have learned to exercise ecological intelligence. Rather, they are based on the same deep cultural assumptions and silences that underlie the liberal ideology that leads to thinking in abstract categories that represents the individual as autonomous, the rational process (and critical inquiry) as free of cultural influences, change as progressive in nature, and that this is a human-centered world. The silences in the thinking of both social justice and market liberals include the lack of awareness of other cultural ways of knowing, how ecological intelligence differs from what both social justice and market liberals assume to be individual intelligence, the importance of the world's diversity of cultural commons as sites of resistance to the market forces that are destroying community patterns of mutual support as well as local ecosystems, and an indifference to how print-based knowledge (now magnified as a cultural shaping force by the increasing reliance upon computers) is both ethnocentric and a colonizing technology. (Bowers, 2012)

Another point needs to be made, and that is by identifying the West's industrial culture as conservative, the followers of Freire and Dewey are able to avoid facing up to the fact that their liberal ideas about the need to emancipate students from what they claim is the oppressive nature of all intergenerational knowledge and traditions, which they consider to be their world-wide mission, makes them complicit in the spread of western hegemony. The educational approaches to transformative learning (Dewey's method of experimental inquiry, Freire's process of conscientization, Giroux's teacher who is to act as a "transformative intellectual"—even in Islamic cultures, McLaren's appeal for a "pedagogical negativism" (that is, to doubt everything) and now for them to become followers of Che Guevara's Marxism, and the professors of education who advocate that students should construct their own knowledge—support the transformative nature of industrial culture in undermining what remains of the world's diverse cultural and natural commons.

The world's diversity of cultural commons, which often include reactionary and morally problematic traditions, may at the same time also serve as cultural sites of resistance to the spread of a consumer-dependent and environmentally destructive lifestyle. This latter possibility is not even considered by the proponents of transformative learning. It is also important to note that both the assumptions and silences that are hallmarks of the formulaic thinking that characterizes today's liberal/ progressive thinking are also taken for granted by the proponents of the UNESCO global agenda of promoting transformative learning and critical inquiry in teacher education programs.

The way in which Moacir Gadotti represents the nature and purpose of transformative learning is particularly important to consider, as he makes the ecological crisis the central focus of his analysis and prescriptions for reform. He claims that just before Freire's death he became aware of the importance of formulating an eco-pedagogy that would address the roots of the crisis, and that he, Gadottti, was simply expanding upon ideas that would lead to the recognition of Freire as a pioneer environmental thinker. As Gadotti did not make available Freire's writings on the nature of an eco-pedagogy, there is no way of verifying Gadotti's claim. But an examination of Gadotti's own writings, as well as the public talk he gave at a recent conference sponsored by the Ontario Institute for the Study of Education reveal that Gadotti has departed in a significant way from Freire's idea of how knowledge is to be transformed. At the same time, Gadotti reproduces both the silences and colonizing hubris that can be traced back to Freire's penchant for interpreting cultural differences as representing different stages in the evolutionary development of cultures.

A key characteristic of Freire's thinking, which Gadotti revises in an even more problematic way, is that there is only one valid approach to knowledge, and that this approach (conscientization roughly interpreted as critical reflection) must lead to a transforming praxis. Learning, as Freire put it, involves a constant renaming of the world of previous generations. In *Pedagogy of the Oppressed* (1974 edition), he writes that "to speak a true word is to transform the world." (p. 75) Thus, humans can only realize their fullest potential as they learn to speak a "true word." To quote Freire again, "To exist humanly, is to name the world, to change it." He goes on to reject the intergenerational knowledge achieved by all the world's cultures by claiming that "once named, the world in its turn reappears as a problem and requires of them a new *naming*." What has become an unquestioned Truth for his many followers around the world is that "men are not built in silence, but in word, in work, in action-reflection." (p. 76, italics in original) Anything other than transformative learning based on critical reflection and the assumption that change is inherently both humanizing and progressive in nature must be viewed as a "banking approach" to learning where the Other transfers (imposes) knowledge that alienates humans from fulfilling their essential nature as makers of history. (1985, p. 199)

In the essay, "Pedagogy of the Earth and Culture of Sustainability" (2000), Gadotti repeats Freire's warning about the dehumanizing nature of the banking approach to learning by quoting Emile Durkheim's warning about turning the process of education into the transmission of culture "from one generation to the next." (p. 8) Gadotti agrees with Freire that, regardless of the differences in cultural knowledge systems which they never consider in any depth, there is only one true approach to knowledge. But he deviates from Freire's position on the emancipatory power of critical reflection and the constant renaming of the world by claiming that an eco-pedagogy can only achieve the goal of creating a planetary consciousness (and thus a planetary citizen) as each individual undertakes "the grand journey... in his interior universe and in the universe that surrounds him." (p. 8) This reformulation is deeply problematic for a number of reasons. The most obvious is that subjectively-based knowledge, which is always influenced by the individual's taken-for-granted cultural assumptions, will not lead to a shared understanding of what is required of a planetary citizen.

Given the evidence today of how people who exercise their rationality within the context of Hindu, Muslim, or Christian cultures, cannot reach agreement in ways that would lead them to give up their own deeply held assumptions about the origins and nature of reality, it would seem that Gadotti would have avoided making the "grand journey" into the interior universe of each individual the basis of an eco-pedagogy. Indeed a strong case can be made that there is no "interior space" that is free of cultural/linguistic influences. That Gadotti would think that the cultural transmission model of learning can be avoided by locating the source of true knowledge in the interior, subjective universe of the individual and in *his* (Gadotti's gender-biased metaphor) subjective interpretation of the surrounding universe indicates that he does not understand how the metaphorical nature of the vocabulary acquired in the early stages of primary socialization reproduces many of the misconceptions, silences, and even wisdom rooted in the narratives of the culture. Even if the "grand journey" of each individual into his/her "interior universe" and the surrounding universe were to be taken there is little likelihood of agreement on what constitutes the responsibilities of a planetary citizen.

Aside from this difference in the way emancipatory knowledge is to be attained, Freire and Gadotti share more than the assumptions about the progressive nature of change, the need to impose on the rest of the world's cultures a single approach to knowledge, and their way of understanding what constitutes the highest expression of human nature. That is, they also share the same silences—which are also reproduced in the thinking of their many followers. The silences include avoiding any recognition of the intergenerational traditions of different cultures that sustain their cultural and natural commons that are sources of empowerment and self-sufficiency within the possibilities and limits of the local bioregions, and that are the basis of the moral codes that govern human/nature relationships. While Gadotti must be credited for his in-depth discussion of the cultural forces that are major contributors to the ecological crisis, he repeats the error of Freire and his followers in not addressing the educational issues that surround the need for students to understand that while socially unjust and ecologically unsustainable practices need to be reformed, there is also a need to become aware of what needs to be conserved as sources of resistance to being colonized by the western project of economic globalization—which constitutes another form of planetary citizenship, but one suited more to the requirements of an industrial/consumer dependent culture.

One of the ironies surrounding the widespread acceptance of the ideas of Freire, Dewey, and now such current proponents of transformative learning as Edmund O'Sullivan, is that they all rely upon evolutionary theory to explain cultural differences. For Dewey and Freire, it is the mainstream Social Darwinism of the last century and a half, while for Gadotti and O'Sullivan it is the Darwinism of Thomas Berry and Brian Swimme. The evolutionary-based hubris of Dewey and Freire can be seen in how they understood the more culturally evolved nature of their respective one-true-approach to knowledge, and in their total indifference to the possibility that we can learn anything about environmentally sustainable practices of cultures Dewey labels as "savages" (1916, pp. 394, 396) and that Freire referred to as backward and living an existence little advanced beyond that of animals.

As this criticism of Freire's may appear as unfair, I shall quote the attributes he associates with different levels of cultural development. In *Education for Critical Consciousness* (1973), he describes the characteristics of the "backward regions of Brazil" in the following way: "men of semi-intransitive consciousness cannot apprehend problems situated outside their sphere of biological necessity. Their interests," he continues, "center almost totally around survival, and they lack a sense of life on a more historical plane." (p. 17) As cultures evolve beyond this near animal state of existence, they move to what he calls "naïve transitivity" where they begin to respond to questions that arise from the context they live in; but their "permeable" state of existence is still limited by their tendency to rely upon polemics and magical explanations. The most evolved cultures are characterized by what Freire calls a "critically transitive consciousness"—which is the state of consciousness with which he identifies himself. The attributes of this state of consciousness include depth in the interpretations of problems, substitution of casual explanations for magical explanations, the practice of dialogue, accepting what is new—and here Freire makes the rare acknowledgement of the need to accept what is good in the old. (p. 18)

Unfortunately, he fails to recognize that this acknowledgement does not fit with his theory about the need for each generation to rename the world and to avoid forms of knowledge that do not emerge from the process of critical reflection. An example of his inability to provide a more balanced understanding of the need for reform as well as the need to renew some forms of intergenerational knowledge can be seen in his discussion of the nature of mentoring—which is a relationship where empowering traditions and skills are intergenerationally renewed in face-to-face relationships. In *Mentoring the Mentor* (1997), Freire suggests the possibility of a more complex understanding of the differences in cultural knowledge systems when he writes "what I am proposing is a profound respect for the cultural identity of students—a cultural identity that implies respect for the language of the other, the color of the other, the gender of the other, the sexual orientation of the other, the intellectual capacity of the other; that implies the ability to stimulate the creativity of the other." (p. 307-308)

This explanation of the role of the mentor suggests that he finally understands the need for a more complex account of the importance of intergenerational renewal in the mentor/mentee relationship, and that it complements the transformative power of critical reflection. But he returns to the mission of promoting the western imperialism that he masks as a liberatory pedagogy that can be traced back to his most seminal book, *Pedagogy of the Oppressed*, when he describes the teacher's role as a mentor. As this is such an important point, it is essential that the reader ask whether the following statement is evidence of Freire's inability to recognize how he subordinates cultural differences to the need to impose a particular set of western cultural assumptions upon others—ironically, in the name of emancipation and dialogue. He writes that

> The fundamental task of the teacher is a liberatory task. It is not to encourage the mentor's goals and aspirations and dreams to be reproduced in the mentees, the students, but to give rise to the possibility that students become owners of their own history. *This is how I understand the need that teachers have to transcend their merely instructive task and to assume the ethical posture of a mentor who truly believes in the total autonomy, freedom, and development of those he or she mentors.* (p. 324, italics added)

What if the traditions of the culture do not include this western Enlightenment ideal of "total" freedom and the autonomous individual? And what if the members of other cultures instead recognize total freedom to be an abstraction of western intellectuals who do not understand the interdependencies and historical continuities that characterize how all individuals are nested in a culture, and how the culture they are linguistically embedded in is nested in the natural systems that sustain life? A possible explanation for why Freire does not recognize this fundamental contradiction that is at the center of his theory of transformative learning is that his evolutionary way of understanding cultural differences leads him to promote what he understands as the most evolved way of thinking.

Gadotti's evolutionary way of thinking is more implicit, yet every bit as imperialistic in intent. Following an insightful critique of how the industrial/capitalistic culture is ravaging the environment, he presents his own vision of how to move from what Thomas Berry and Brian Swimme refer to as the technozoic phase of evolution to the life-sustaining ecozoic phase. Like Freire and Dewey, he proposes a single approach to knowledge: that is, the grand journey into each individual's interior universe. It is important to note that Gadotti anticipates the possibility of criticism for his recommendation that the world's cultural diversity is to be replaced by what he refers to as a "planetary citizenship, a planetary civilization, a *planetary* consciousness." (p. 2. italics in original) Thus, he argues that "globalization in itself does not pose problems, since it constitutes an unprecedented process of advancement in the history of humankind." (p. 8) It is interesting to note here that scientists and techno-utopians whose hubris has led them into the morass of scientism also explain that natural selection is leading to a global culture that will be based on the better adapted culture memes. (Bowers, 2012)

Gadotti also shares with these futurist thinkers the vision that the next stage in globalization will be characterized by cooperation and solidarity. In effect, Gadotti leaves the reader with the idea that the "invisible hand" of natural selection that supposedly guides the transition of cultures from the stage of conflict and aggression to the higher stage where the elimination of differences leads automatically to solidarity will be activated by the grand subjective journey of individuals who are no longer influenced by the cultures they are born into. It is important to remind readers, before they become mesmerized by this oft-repeated western vision of entering a secular paradise where capitalists yield to their critics, and the neo-liberal corporate culture is also working to achieve a planetary consciousness but one that shares the same dependency upon industrially processed food, health care, entertainment, and that finds consumerism as the highest goal in life.

It is important to acknowledge that the rise of liberal/ Enlightenment ideas in the late 18th and 19th century led to basic improvements in the lives of the people of Western Europe who had been oppressed by feudal ideas and institutions—and by the authoritarian political systems that were equally resistant to change. The emphasis on the authority and power of critical reflection to overturn unjust traditions, the idea that change can lead to social progress, the view of the individual as having the power of self-determination, and the idea that new forms of knowledge will mitigate the ravages of the illness and the stultifying nature of work, led to important advances. But it also needs to be kept in mind that the widespread acceptance in the West of these ideas also coincided with the rise of the Industrial Revolution. And more importantly, these liberal ideas had no self-limiting principle. That is, the dominant motivation has been to achieve more and faster progress, more reliance on critical reflection (increasingly exercised by experts promoting the development of new technologies and markets), more labor saving technologies (and now the elimination of the need for workers), newer drugs (and the control of the American Congress to ensure the growing dominance of the drug industry), and more self-determination—including self-determination in the construction of knowledge and values. The lack of any self-limiting principles, which made these liberal ideas even more problematic when they were merged with the market liberalism of John Locke, Adam Smith, and, later, Herbert Spencer, becomes especially evident when we consider the current drive to turn every aspect of the environmental and cultural commons into market opportunities—and to convert the entire world to a survival-of-the-fittest business mentality.

To reiterate a point that I have been making in the earlier part of this critique: in basing their interpretations of transformative learning on these liberal assumptions Dewey, Freire, and Gadotti, as well as the current group of critical pedagogy fundamentalists not only reproduce the contradictions that arise when relying on abstract ideas for reforming a culturally diverse world, but they also reproduce in their interpretations of transformative learning the silences that characterized the earlier phase of liberal/Enlightenment thinking. These silences still contribute to ignoring the differences in cultural ways of knowing as well as the diversity of the intergenerational knowledge that was the basis of community self-sufficiency and mutual support before the Industrial

Revolution made existence dependent upon participating in a money economy. In reality, it was not really a case of ignoring these differences. Rather, in the early phase of liberal thinking it was a matter of viewing other cultures as primitive, uncivilized, and as heathens that needed to be turned into Christians.

The deficit model of cultures has in more recent times been revised so that they are now viewed a pre-literate, pre-scientific, economically and technologically undeveloped, limited by a spectator approach to knowledge, and locked into a semi-intransitive state of consciousness. One of the ironies of viewing literacy as the primary evidence of having achieved a minimal level of civilized existence is that it reinforces the abstract patterns of thinking associated with encoding knowledge in the printed word, and in the process undermining awareness of what Bateson refers to as the "differences which make a difference": that is, the information circulating through all cultural and natural ecosystems. Unlike print, which marginalizes awareness of differences in the lived cultural patterns and local contexts, the oral traditions require giving closer attention to the changes (differences which make a difference) between the participants in local contexts. The differences between oral and print-based storage and thinking, which Dewey, Freire, Gadotti, and their followers have ignored, have been more fully explained in the writings of Jack Goody, Eric Havelock, and Walter Ong. What their writings bring into focus is how the metaphors of "transformation," "emancipation," "progress," as well as Freire's claim that everybody should rename the world of the previous generation (as if this is possible), and Gadotti's claim that true knowledge will emerge from exploring the individual's subjective "interior universe," are all examples of abstract thinking which has been until recently one of the dominant traditions of western philosophers.

The reductionist ways in which various traditions of liberal thinking have categorized non-western cultures, as well as marginalized cultures in the West, have led to ignoring the need for an in-depth understanding of their approaches to knowledge and intergenerational renewal. This reductionist way of thinking, as I have been arguing, is part of the reason for the imperialist orientation of transformative learning theorists such as Dewey, Freire, and Gadotti, and the professors of education who are now promoting transformative learning in non-western countries. More importantly, this bias which shows up in the messianic nature of transformative learning theorists should also be understood as one of the reasons that, when theorists such as Gadotti, O'Sullivan, and McLaren address environmental issues, their panacea is to promote the global acceptance of even more culturally uninformed interpretations of liberal and Marxist ideals. That is, their response to the industrial culture that is accelerating the rate of change in the Earth's natural systems, and in making the people of the world more dependent upon consumerism, is to promote more change through an approach to education that fosters a rootless form of individualism. This condition of cultural amnesia is now being furthered by the changes in consciousness resulting from the increased reliance by youth on Internet communication and thinking. (Carr. 2011)

But they add to the crises of the cultural and environmental commons that is spreading around the world in other ways. Their uncritical embrace of various current versions of Social Darwinism, the oppressive (banking) nature of all cultural models of learning other than their own, the messianic drive to share (impose) their highest ideals on other cultures, the effort to enable other cultures to achieve a western interpretation of what constitutes the fullest expression of their humanity, and so forth—all lead to thinking of other cultures as fundamentally deficient and thus, as Derek Rasmussen points out, in need of being rescued. (Bowers, Apffel-Marglin, pp. 115-131) This way of thinking does not take account of the fact that there are nearly 6000 languages still spoken in the world today—with a third of them in danger of becoming extinct in the near future.

Conserving this diversity in language/knowledge systems is directly related to conserving biological diversity, as many of these languages encode knowledge accumulated over many generations of living in one place and from observing the interdependent relationships that make up the natural and cultural ecology. Unfortunately, transformative learning theorists have not become a voice for educational reforms that support linguistic and, by extension, biological diversity. As long as they maintain their core ideas about learning being only a transformative/emancipatory experience, any references to the importance of cultural diversity is simply empty rhetoric that has as its real purpose the need to represent educational reform agendas as being on the politically correct side of the social justice and environmental debate.

In effect, Freire and the other transformative learning theorists should be understood as being subjects of the banking process of education that they reject for others. That is, their professors imposed upon them a restricted political language that neither they nor their professors have thought critically about. And one of the primary characteristic of this political language, which I have earlier identified with classical liberalism (sans Adams Smith's emphasis on the progressive nature of a market economy) is that it lacks a vocabulary for naming those aspects of culture that are now the only real source of resistance to the imperialism of market liberalism. It is especially noteworthy that the phrases "cultural commons" and "natural commons" are not part of the emancipatory liberal discourse. The problem with the language of liberalism can be seen in Gadotti's way of addressing the ecological crisis. Globalizing the romantic idea of a planetary consciousness emerging from the grand journey into the individual's subjective universe simply does not address the genuine sources of resistance to economic globalization and its impact on natural systems.

From the beginning of human history the cultural commons have represented the legacy, which some refer to as the gift economy, that now takes on special importance as alternatives to living the double bind of being dependent upon consumerism in an era of growing unemployment. The nature of the commons varies from culture to culture, and from bioregion to bioregion. What makes the cultural commons a gift economy is that much of the culture's symbolic patterns, skills, mentoring relationships, as well as the natural systems of the bioregion, are available to the members of the community on a largely non-monetary basis. That is, they have not been enclosed—that is, privatized, commodified, monetized, incorporated into an industrial process, and so forth. This gift economy is also free from government taxes, and the threat of inflation and deflation.

This general account of the commons does not mean that all of the culturally diverse commons where or are currently free of political systems that give certain groups special advantages—including the right to restrict the commons to the bare essentials for sustaining life. To make the point more directly, the commons should not be understood as always free of status systems and the unequal use of power. On the other hand, many of the cultural commons have been and still are characterized by local decision-making—an important phenomenon that is now being undermined by the World Trade Organization and capitalist-driven forms of enclosure where decisions about the use of the commons are now made by corporate and private owners who are not adversely affected by their decisions. The enclosure (privatization) of municipal water systems, as well as the corporate ownership and sale of supposedly "pure" bottled water, are examples of how the process of enclosing the commons also undermines local democracy.

In terms of the discussion of the relevance of transformative learning theories for addressing the ecological crisis, what is important to consider is how the liberal discourse of Freire, Dewey, Gadotti, and the critical and eco-pedagogy fundamentalists (Henry Giroux, Peter McLaren, and their current followers) lack the language for representing in other than pejorative terms what is distinctive about the commons. This includes their inability to recognize that the commons are dependent upon intergenerational knowledge which can also be understood as traditions. As mentioned earlier, the word tradition has a pejorative meaning for all of the transformative learning theorists even though they are themselves entirely dependent upon the re-enactment of traditions in their use of language and most other areas of their daily lives. By associating intergenerational knowledge with oppression (and some of it is oppressive), and in not recognizing the many ways different cultures encode and renew their traditions of intergenerational knowledge and skill for living less consumer dependent lives, these transformative learning theorists are unable to clarify how the revitalization of the commons of various communities in North America, and in other parts of the world, are sites of resistance to economic globalization.

The implications of the transformative learning theorists' collective silences and reductionist thinking is that they have nothing to say about the need to re-direct curriculum reform in ways that help students recognize the different aspects of the commons that are otherwise taken for granted. In not being given the language for naming and thus making explicit their cultural commons experiences, they will be unable to recognize and thus challenge politically when the commons are being further enclosed. That is, in addition to not understanding their rights within their cultural and natural commons, as well as their responsibility to future generations for ensuring that the commons are not further diminished by corporate capitalism, their present exposure to the modernizing agenda of education (which will become even more limited as transformative learning becomes more widespread) now leaves them largely ignorant of the non-monetized face-to-face alternatives within their communities to consumerism.

The other irony is that the use of the restrictive liberal political vocabulary that the transformative learning theorists reinforce in teacher education classes, which in turn is reinforced in public schools, is that in America a significant number of people now call themselves conservatives while supporting the imperialistic assumptions and practices of market liberals. This has the effect of social and ecojustice advocates not wanting to identify themselves with the word conservatism. The result is that both the faux conservatives and the transformative learning theorists support each other in avoiding the question that now needs to be ask in this era of economic and cultural colonization: namely, what do we need to conserve in order to resist the forces that are increasing poverty around the world and putting future generations at greater risk of an environment that is too contaminated to support a healthy and fulfilling life.

The challenge will be for the current generation of transformative learning theorists to recognize how they have been indoctrinated by liberal ideologues who failed to renew what was viable in the earlier formulations of liberal ideas in ways that address issues related to the diversity of the world's cultural commons and the environmental changes of which the earlier liberal theorists were unaware.

As the ecological/cultural crises deepens, and more international organizations such as UNESCO, as well as the various national groups such as the American Association for Sustainability in Higher Education, take a more leading role in promoting ecologically sustainable educational reforms, it is absolutely essential that Albert Einstein's warning be taken seriously: namely, that the same mind-set that created the problems cannot be relied upon to fix them. This is the double bind now faced by all educational reformers. By borrowing ideas from educational theorists who were ethnocentric thinkers, and who shared the deep cultural assumptions that underlie the West's long tradition of cultural colonization, Einstein's warning will likely go unheeded. This is clearly evident in educational reforms being promoted by UNESCO, and in the inability of faculty across the disciplines to recognize that the silences of the professors who guided their graduate studies in the last decades of the 20th century left them with the same mind-set that is exacerbating the ecological/cultural crises.

When graduate students borrow the ideas of theorists from other cultures they are not likely to be informed that the print-based knowledge and thinking widely represented as the basis of progressive thinking is inherently ethnocentric and abstract in ways that marginalize awareness of the ecologically sustainable practices within local cultures. In short, the process of cultural colonization that occurs from a university education, particularly in the West, is often hidden by the success in achieving a doctoral degree and gaining access to a university teaching and research position. When students return to their home country, they too often become promoters of the West's ecologically unsustainable patterns of thinking. And as elite universities in the West increasingly offer their degrees online, this process of cultural colonization to the environmentally destructive patterns of past ways of thinking, as well as the silences about the cultural and environmental commons, will continue to go unchallenged.

The critical question that needs to be asked about the educational reform agenda of the UNESCO theorists, which is so clearly supportive of colonizing students in other cultures to patterns of thinking that will make them more dependent upon a consumer lifestyle, is the following: Is their support of transformative learning and critical pedagogy as the basis of education for sustainable development (to use their code words) based on a deep understanding of why other cultural ways of knowing must now be overturned, or do they promote these supposedly progressive and emancipatory ways of learning because they are unaware of the cultural differences between ecologically sustainable and unsustainable practices and beliefs? A further question that needs to be asked is: Do they understand the nature of ecological intelligence, and how it is expressed differently in other cultures? Given the nature of the global educational reforms they are proposing, the answers should be obvious. Unfortunately, the silences in their graduate studies have left them unable to think outside of the paradigm certified by the awarding of a graduate degree. This is a far more difficult problem to address, and it is likely that the rate of environmental degradation will not allow us the time necessary for bringing about the needed change in consciousness. The hubris that accompanies the missionary drive to transform and thus emancipate cultures from their supposed less evolved state of consciousness makes it even more difficult to take seriously the consequences that will follow from ignoring Einstein's warning.

References

Carr, Nicholas. 2011. *The Shallows: What the Internet is Doing to Our Brains.* New York: W.W. Norton

Bowers, C. A. 1983."Linguistic Roots of Cultural Invasion in Paulo Freire's Pedagogy." Reprinted in 1993, in *Critical Essays on Education, Modernity, and the Recovery of the Ecological Imperative.* New York: Teachers College Press, pp. 34-52.

_____. 2001. *Educating for Eco-Justice and Community.* Athens, Georgia: University of Georgia Press.

_____. 2003. *Mindful Conservatism: Rethinking the Ideological and Educational Basis of an Ecologically Sustainable Future.* Lanham, Maryland: Rowman & Littlefield.

_____. 2005. *The False Promises of Constructivist Theories of Learning: A Global and Ecological Critique.* New York: Peter Lang.

_____. 2011. *Perspectives on the Ideas of Gregory Bateson, Ecological Intelligence, and Educational Reforms.* Eugene, OR.: Eco-Justice Press.

_____. 2012. *The Way Forward: Educational Reforms that Focus on the Cultural Commons and the Linguistic Roots of the Ecological/Cultural Crises.* Eugene, OR: Eco-Justice Press.

Bowers, C. A. and Frederique Apffel Marglin (editors). 2005. *Rethinking Freire: Globalization and the Environmental Crisis.* Mahawh, N.J.: Lawrence Erlbaum.

Dewey, John. 1916. *Democracy and Education.* New York: Macmillan.

Freire, Paulo. 1973. *Education for Critical Consciousness.* New York: Seabury Press.

_____. 1974 edition. *Pedagogy of the Oppressed.* New York: Seabury Press.

_____. 1985. *The Politics of Education: Culture, Power, and Liberation.* South Hadley, MA.: Bergin & Garvey.

_____. 1997. *Mentoring the Mentor: A Critical Dialogue with Paulo Freire.* New York: Peter Lang.

Gadotti, Moacir. 2000. "Pedagogy of the Earth and Culture of Sustainability." Sao Paulo, Brazil. Instituto Paulo Freire. Pp. 2-11

Goody, Jack. 1987. *The Interface Between the Written and the Oral.* Cambridge, U.K.: Cambridge University Press.

Havelock, Eric. 1986. *The Muse Learns to Write: Reflections on Orality and Literacy from Antiquity to the Present.* New Haven, Conn.: Yale University Press.

Ong, Walter. 1982. *Orality and Literacy: The Technologizing of the Word.* London: Methuen.

Rasmussen, Derek. 1995. "Cease to Do Evil, Then Learn to Do Good (A Pedagogy of the Oppressor." In *Rethinking Freire: Globalization and the Environmental Crisis*, edited by C. A. Bowers and Frederique Apffel-Marglin. Mahwah, N.J.: Lawrence Erlbaum Associates.

Chapter 3

Language Issues that Should be the Central Focus in Teacher Education and Curriculum Studies

The current generation of teacher educators and curriculum studies professors, like their colleagues in other disciplines across the university, continue to perpetuate the cultural lag that is leading to yet another generation of academics who will reproduce the misconceptions and silences that represented the high-status knowledge taken for granted in the last decades of the 20th century. This was an era still dominated by many of the deep cultural assumptions about individualism, progress, the efficacy of the rational process and critical thinking, and American exceptionalism that gave conceptual direction and moral legitimacy to the industrial/consumer-dependent culture that is being globalized as part of the modernizing agenda. This era included social justice oriented liberal academics in colleges of education who focused on multiculturalism, gender, racial, and homophobic prejudices and practices of exclusion. My criticism is not that these are not the right issues to be taken into account, but that these issues were framed in ways that excluded consideration of what scientists had been reporting about the rapid rate of environmental degradation.

Given the continued silence on the part of social justice educators it is important to note that the last decades of the 20th century was not an era when environmental issues were of interest only to scientists. Richard Nixon used his presidential address to declare that the 1970s were the "environmental decade." With bipartisan support 23 pieces of environmental legislation were passed, with full coverage by the press. Earlier, in 1962, Rachel Carson's *Silent Spring* received national attention, as did the Club of Rome Report, *The Limits of Growth* which appeared in 1972. Unfortunately, academics across the disciplines, with the exception of certain areas of science, ignored these early efforts to address the growing ecological crisis. Their silence supported the assumption that changes in natural systems, as well as their restoration, were the responsibility of scientists—which was a view encouraged by scientists who were in denial about the cultural roots of the ecological crisis. Then and now, the cultural beliefs and practices, particularly the modernizing/Enlightenment agenda being promoted by academics across the disciplines, including by teacher educators and curriculum studies professors, were not seen as contributing forces.

Unfortunately, the majority of teacher education and curriculum studies professors, who did their graduate work during the last decades of the 20th century, continue to perpetuate the silences and double bind thinking of their professors. That is, they continue to promote the same deep cultural modernizing assumptions that were constituted before there was an awareness of environmental limits even as they promote social justice educational reform—particularly reforms that promote greater individual autonomy and access to the middle class world of consumerism. For most academics, Gregory Bateson's *Steps to an Ecology of Mind* (1972) was difficult to understand because it challenged so many of the misconceptions that had been reinforced for generations in universities—indeed, in some instances, for centuries. This was the book that should have awakened these social justice educators, as well as academics across the university, to the importance of how the metaphorical vocabulary inherited from earlier eras marginalized awareness of environmental limits and that the ecological crisis was also a crisis in cultural ways of knowing.

The silences and denials of the last decades of the 20th century continue to dominate the thinking of the majority of teacher educators and curriculum studies professors. One has only to look at the title of papers presented at professional conferences, such as the American Educational Research Association, the American Educational Studies Association, and other specialized conferences for teacher educators, educational philosophers, and environmental educators. The group advocating an eco-pedagogy approach to educational reforms, who are attempting to reconcile the ideas of Paulo Freire with an awareness of ecologically sustainable cultural practices, as well as those advocating curricular changes that meet the guiding principles of ecojustice, represent a small minority that is likely to be overwhelmed by the growing national sentiment that the environmental crisis is a liberal hoax. What is generally ignored are the economic interests of those in denial, which can be recognized by examining their educational goals for the country: the core market liberal values of individualism, a consumer-dependent lifestyle, unending technological progress, free-markets, a human-centered world, and the globalization of the American model of development.

Much of culture is learned at a taken for granted level where the patterns are experienced as both normal, natural, and constantly reinforced by what other people of the same cultural group take for granted. Thus, most of our cultural knowledge is tacit and beyond critical reflection. This process accounts for several of the dominant characteristics in courses taken as part of the professional studies in colleges of education. The two most important include the following:

The Survey Approach:

Courses that engage students in discussing a wide variety of readings is a hang-over from what current professors of education learned from their mentors in the late decades of the 20th century. The main themes of the course—which range from reading issues, learning theories, multiculturalism, history and philosophy of education, environmental education and even to eco-pedagogy and ecojustice oriented courses—reflect the personal interests of the professor and the continuing influence of her/his graduate school mentors.

Unfortunately, the two most critically important drawbacks of a survey course is that it seldom provides for an in-depth understanding of the conceptual underpinnings of the readings to which students are being introduced. The second drawback is that it perpetuates the silences about how current theories of learning, educational reforms that focus on social justice issues, approaches to using computers in the classroom, and so forth, fail to address the various ways in which the processes of cultural reproduction perpetuate the assumptions that lead to ecologically unsustainable lifestyles. For example, how many survey courses in the areas of reading, learning theory, multicultural education, and even environmental education, introduce students to a deep understanding of how the metaphorical nature of the vocabulary carries forward earlier patterns of thinking that are totally out of touch with today's world? How many courses on the educational uses of computers, for example, introduce students to the literature on how literacy and orality affect, in profoundly different ways, consciousness, identities, and patterns of social organization? How many science and environmental education courses introduce students to how scientists continue to take for granted the meta-cognitive schemata (the root metaphors such as progress and a human-centered world) that led them to introduce the synthetic chemicals that are now altering all forms of life—and to think of their achievements as expressions of how they are contributing to progress in bringing the environment under scientific control? How many courses focused on reading and learning theories inform students about why print-based learning may make learning difficult for students who come from oral dominated cultures where abstract thinking is not privileged? How many students in philosophy of education courses learn that the major western philosophers were with few exceptions ethnocentric thinkers who were also clueless about the cultural commons that represented the everyday practices that reduce dependence upon consumerism while providing alternatives to the capitalist approach to work which is now shedding the need for workers?

Students who have taken the survey social justice courses where the ideas of John Dewey and Paulo Freire are introduced as the basis of progressive and thus emancipatory thinking, as I have personally observed, are unaware of why both theorists are Social Darwinian and ethnocentric thinkers, and totally unaware of how the core cultural assumptions that inform their approaches to social reform undermine the culturally diverse cultural and environmental commons. In short, survey courses fail to provide the depth of understanding about how various pedagogical and curriculum extrapolations may be based on deeper cultural patterns that were not understood in the first place. To make this point more directly, survey courses too often lead to superficial thinking and thus to a reliance on formulaic thinking and clichés, and to being unable to challenge the conceptual orthodoxies held within the larger society.

The Tendency to Ride One's Own Horse:

This phenomenon is widely practiced not only by professors of education, but by academics across the disciplines. That is, faculty tend to pursue a particular line of inquiry, including the depth of literature that informs the chosen area of inquiry. This tradition is a key contributor to the cultural lag where current professors reproduce the same "riding one's own horse" pattern of thinking they learned from their mentors. This pattern is especially problematic as it too often leads to indoctrinating unsuspecting students with the area of knowledge that the professor, for a variety of reasons, is most deeply invested in. It's not that students do not learn from professors who are focused primarily on gender, racial, homophobic, social class, and other issues that fit under the label of transformative learning. The personal interests of the professor may be important, but too often they are presented in a missionary spirit that limits students from encountering other perspectives and, again, from encountering the dominant issues that the entire world now faces— which are the changes in natural systems that are increasing the misery of hundreds of millions of people. The tendency to ride one's own horse is reinforced by the need to publish in order to be promoted through the ranks, and to establish one's prominence within the field. Given these pressures, what is both easiest and safest is to continue to focus on a narrow area of specialization. The problem for students, as well as for the larger society that needs radical thinkers who can both challenge the too often taken for granted cultural orthodoxies, as well as suggest viable alternatives to the cultural practices that are pushing us beyond sustainable limits, is that the benefits of riding one's own horse are seen as outweighing the importance of learning about what one's chosen paradigm cannot address.

Both the survey courses and the intellectual avoidance that accompanies riding one's own horse are obstacles to learning what was not understood by the majority of academics in the years following World War II. As I have pointed out elsewhere, the scholarship that is now beginning to be recognized as having important implications for understanding why colleges of education and most academic disciplines continue to avoid addressing the cultural roots of the ecological crisis was just beginning to appear within different disciplines in the 1970s and 80s. And this scholarship, including the writings of Michael Reddy, Eric Havelock, Jack Goody, and Walter Ong on the orality/literacy issues, Gregory Bateson's challenge to the idea of individual intelligence and his insights about the role of historically constituted language in perpetuating double bind thinking, went against the widely accepted convention of treating language as a conduit for communicating objective ideas and information. Their ideas, as well as recognizing that both cultural and natural systems need to be understood as ecologies, that the cultural commons represent perhaps the only viable alternative to the industrial/consumer-dependent lifestyle, and that computers and other technologies are not culturally neutral and thus are not an inherent expression of progress, represent the intellectual challenges of the 21st century.

Perhaps the more critical question today is whether faculty outside of the sciences and those within the various disciplines who frame environmental issues within the conceptual traditions of their discipline (which is itself limiting), are aware of the disruptive environmental changes that lie in the immediate decades ahead. And secondly, do they care enough to move beyond the security of their chosen area of scholarship and teaching to begin questioning the orthodoxies of the last centuries that each generation has updated but not radically changed? Are they ready to address the questions relating to the knowledge and skills students need to acquire if they are to learn how to grow and prepare their own food, live in ways that do not assume that water is in infinite supply, and to learn from the local cultural commons how to discover and develop talents that reduce dependence upon consumerism? Are faculty still rooted in late 20th century thinking prepared to help students recognize the various ways in which the market system, media and thus corporate controlled silences, undermine awareness of alternatives to the consumer-dependent lifestyles? Are they able to help students understand how digital technologies are contributing to the myth of individualism and the accompanying state of cultural amnesia? Do they recognize the cultural patterns that continue to reinforce the myth of the autonomous exercise of individual intelligence, and can they help students recognize the differences when they are exercising ecological intelligence? Can they provide students the conceptual framework for understanding why a wider reliance upon the exercise of ecological intelligence is essential for making the transition to an ecologically sustainable future? These may appear as challenges that are too daunting, especially when past traditions of graduate studies have not prepared current academics to understand these issues—much less recognize the pedagogical and curricular implications.

Where to Begin, and How to Involve Students in 21st Century Learning and Daily Practices?

Regardless of the specialized area of interest—from becoming a reading specialist, English or social studies teacher, an environmental educator, a math and physics teacher—all teachers will be dependent upon the cultural processes seldom addressed directly in teacher education and graduate educational studies programs. For that matter, the education of academics in other disciplines, with only a few exceptions, perpetuate the same silences. Largely ignored are the different languaging processes that reproduce a culture's taken for granted ways of knowing, values, and understanding of human and nature relationships. There is, in short, no area of the curriculum that does not rely upon the languaging systems of the culture, or that of other cultures. Yet learning about these processes, what they hide, what they distort, when they become sources of empowerment, and, more importantly, when they contribute to cultural changes that may reduce the culture's adverse impact on natural systems, are seldom part of the classroom teacher and professor's professional studies.

When as a member of the faculty at the University of Oregon I tried to introduce this major shortcoming in the teacher education program I was told that I should understand that since everybody uses language to communicate their ideas there was nothing further that needed to be studied. They were thinking of language as a conduit in a sender/receiver process of sending ideas, data, and information to others—which is the view of language reinforced in the use of textbooks, in computer-mediated communication and software programs, in lectures, in power-point presentations, and in most daily conversations. Unfortunately, this view of language is incorrect, and is a major reason why so little attention is given in educational settings to how the deep ecologically problematic cultural assumptions formed in the distant past continue to be passed from generation to generation. Given the long progressive tradition of educators urging students to construct their own knowledge, which a large segment of the public is now doing in ways that threaten the historical foundations of our democracy, there is even less awareness of the range of language issues that teachers and professors should be addressing beyond those relating to gender, racial, and homophobic discrimination.

In a recent course I taught at the University of Oregon, I avoided introducing students to a survey of readings that address curriculum issues, as I knew they would encounter these surveys in other courses. I also avoided the mistake made in a newly established computers in education course where students were asked to come up with their own reading list. By not knowing the issues relating to the cultural non-neutrality of computer-mediated learning, or the questions that should be asked about the ideology encoded in software programs, the students presented 20 minute summaries that reproduced most of the silences that exist in the current educational discourse about the advantages of relying upon computers in the classroom. They were pleased to be in control of their own learning, but were totally unaware of the questions and conceptual frameworks necessary for understanding what they need to bring to the attention of students about the cultural non-neutrality of computers and digital communication in general.

My many years of challenging what I earlier referred to as the culture of denial has led to the conviction that teacher education courses, as well as those I taught in the Honors College and the Center for Environmental Studies, should introduce students to what they do not know: that is, the cultural silences perpetuated in classrooms and through the media. The course described below thus avoids introducing students to past theorists who wrote about different approaches to educational reforms that were relevant in earlier days but totally irrelevant in terms addressing today's issues. It also avoids what too many students now expect: to control what they learn and to not be too intellectually challenged. Given the narcissistic mind-set of many of their professors, these expectations seem on the surface to be praiseworthy yet naïve in a world facing environmental and cultural challenges not encountered before. The following is how the students were introduced to an in-depth understanding of the langauging processes that are unavoidable in making pedagogical and curricular decisions. It also presents the core concepts that students in professional education courses should encounter before taking other courses—especially survey courses. The justification for this claim is that the concepts explored in depth in the course lead to recognizing the 20th century legacy of misconceptions and silences that will be encountered in the specialized courses in teacher education and in other disciplines across the university.

EDST 610 *Curriculum Reform for a Sustainable Future*
Overview of Course:

In taking Albert Einstein's observation seriously that the same mind-set that created the problem cannot be relied upon to fix it, this course will have four main foci. **First**, *it will reframe the current approaches to thinking about curriculum reform in ways that take account of the cultural/linguistic patterns of thinking and relationships that contribute to a smaller ecological footprint, and to lifestyle changes that address the growing unemployment due to the further automation of the workplace. Special attention will be given to what teachers need to understand about how the language in the curriculum and in classroom discussions often reproduces the misconceptions of an earlier era when environmental limits were not understood. How to help students recognize when it is important to reframe the meaning of words in ways that are culturally and ecologically informed will also be given attention.* **Second**, *attention will be given to how curriculum reform can help students recognize the connections between a consumer-dependent lifestyle and the deepening ecological crises. The nature and ecological importance of the local cultural commons (the intergenerational knowledge, skills, and mentoring relationships that are less dependent upon consumerism) will also be considered, as well as the teacher's role in helping students become more aware of the differences in their personal development and the ecological impact as they move between the relationships and activities within the local cultural commons and settings where they are consumers.* **Third**, *attention will be given to what students need to understand about how computer-mediated learning contributes to a smaller ecological footprint within certain contexts as well as how it undermines the local cultural commons. How to incorporate into the curriculum an understanding of the cultural transforming characteristics of computers will also be addressed.* **Fourth**, *attention will be given to how to understand the nature of ecological intelligence, and how it differs from the myth of individual intelligence that is reinforced in most classrooms as well as in print-based forms of communication. Understanding these core issues will also be sources of empowerment in other work settings.*

This approach to introducing future teachers to the core issues in their profession avoids treating the language issues in the abstract or only in terms of social justice issues. The main focus was on the wide range of issues that are ignored because of the conduit view of language that is dominant in so many areas of discourse (both written and spoken). The discussion also focused on curricular approaches that would enable their students to recognize how language shapes their own experiences in ways that challenge the long-held assumption that autonomous thinking individuals use language to communicate their ideas to others—and that there is such a thing as objective knowledge and facts. These are among the most important misconceptions that classroom teachers must know how to address in ways that take into account ethnic differences as well as the even greater challenge of enabling students to recognize the role that language plays in deepening the ecological crisis. Bateson's insight that understanding relationships rather than focusing on individual entities was used as the basis for putting the teachers' professional knowledge on an ecological footing.

That is, the four major conceptual categories mentioned in the description of the course were presented as ecologies—the ecology of languaging processes, the ecology of the tension between the cultural commons and a consumer-dependent lifestyle, the ecology of computer-mediated learning and abstract thinking, and the ecology of moving to different levels in exercising ecological intelligence. One of the implications of reframing what is being suggested here as the conceptual areas that should be part of the basis of the teacher's professional knowledge is a characteristic of all cultural and natural ecologies: namely, that relationships within micro and macro ecological systems have a history, are sustained though complex patterns of message exchanges, and that both their history and current patterns of interaction and interdependence have implications for their future prospects. These relationships are essential for thinking about the ecology of language, of the cultural commons, of the print/computer/Internet patterns of storage and communication, and of the process of exercising ecological intelligence.

The discussions on curriculum reform, particularly those that focused on the pedagogical and curricular implications, stressed that helping students to think ecologically requires that they take into account the history of ideas, words, events, technological developments and so forth—as well as how they affect current patterns of interaction and mutual support, as well as their implications for the future. These simple and common sense guidelines for thinking, as discussed in the class, brought into question the current emphasis (largely driven by testing and most teachers' past socialization) that there are objective facts, that events and ideas can be understood in terms of cause and effect, and that abstract ideas and accounts of events have universal relevance. The following represent the key concepts that were discussed in the course, with a major focus being on how the concepts can be introduced to public school and university students. It was emphasized that the concepts should be reframed as questions to be investigated in term of the student's own cultural contexts. In addition to the importance of the concepts, question-directed inquiry encourages students to give close attention to cultural patterns they might otherwise take for granted. The questions, when raised in the classroom, are really a matter of naming what previously was un-named and thus not made explicit. And when made explicit, the connections between otherwise taken for granted cultural patterns can then be examined in terms of their consequences on other patterns. Understanding the patterns that connect, as Bateson reminds us, is learning to think ecologically. This process then needs to be extended to examining how the student's taken for granted cultural patterns of thought and behavior affects the ecology of relationships within the natural systems. Indeed, this might be easier for younger students to do than adults whose ideas and patterns of behavior have become habituated.

Ecology of Languaging Processes:
1. Words have a history (which is a basic insight that leads to classroom discussions of the following curricular possibilities)
2. Most words are metaphors that encode the analogs settled upon in earlier times and thus carry forward the insights, misconceptions, and silences of the earlier state of cultural awareness. (Student conducted interviews will yield short term perspectives on how the meaning of words have changed, and the Online Etymological Dictionary will provide a long-term perspective on how the meaning of words have changed over time—and been influenced by other linguistic traditions)
3. When born into the metaphorical language of a language community, the initial process of thinking is influenced by the historically constituted meanings that others took for granted. That is, acquiring the language of one's community also involves being dependent upon ways of thinking about issues and problems that were unknown in earlier times.

4. This disconnect between past ways of thinking and current ecological realities is the basis of double bind thinking.
5. The taken for granted ways in which people rely upon past ways of thinking, even while thinking that their ideas and values are individually determined, are a dominant characteristic of the curriculum—whether spoken or read.
6. Most curricula and most patterns of verbal communication reinforce a conduit view of language where supposedly objective ideas and data, or an individual's own ideas, are passed to others.
7. The conduit view of language, which is reinforced in print and thus in computer-mediated cultural storage and communication, hides the basic reality that words have a history—as well as how they carry forward earlier culturally specific ways of thinking, misconceptions, prejudices, and silences.
8. The conduit view of languaging processes hides how words, as metaphors, encode earlier and culturally specific analogs that contribute to the linguistic colonization of the present by the past, and to the colonization of other cultures.
9. Words can be given new meanings when the choice of analogs is informed by other cultural ways of knowing and a knowledge of current environmental changes.
10. Learning about the history of words, as well as considering whether the analogs derived from earlier ways of thinking are adequate for understanding and responding to current cultural and environmental issues, will enable a diverse student group to understand both the linguistic colonization of the present by the past as well as the linguistic colonization of students learning to speak English.

Ecology of the Cultural Commons:
1. The cultural commons involve the daily practices that are based on intergenerational knowledge, skills, and patterns of mutual support that rely less on a money economy.
2. The cultural commons exist in every community and the activities range from food preparation and sharing, healing practices, patterns of mutual support, ceremonies, games that depend upon the rules handed down from the past, creative arts and craft skills

that rely upon mentoring, a heritage of knowledge of place, civil liberties, knowledge about the care for animals, how to build a dwelling, to live by values and skills that have a small impact on the land, and so forth

3. Cultural commons activities bring people together in interdependent relationships, and lead to discovery of personal talents and skills.

4. The cultural commons, that is the intergenerational knowledge that enabled pre-industrial people to survive, grow in population, and to expand their knowledge and patterns of self-governance, began with the first humans wandering the savannas of what we now call Africa.

5. The cultural commons involve a more complex economy of mutual exchange, barter, and volunteerism, and thus provides for alternative community-centered lifestyles in an era of increasing automation driven unemployment and economic uncertainties.

6. Most cultural commons activities have a smaller toxic and carbon impact on natural systems

7. The cultural commons are as diverse as the world's cultures and bioregions.

8. Practices within the cultural commons more often involve local decision making, and a sense of making decisions that strengthen community—rather than decisions based on the pursuit of self-interest, competition, and more profits.

9. Public schools and universities tend to marginalize awareness of the local cultural commons by emphasizing abstract thinking (that is, print-based knowledge) as well as the values and assumptions that underlie an individualistic, progressive, and consumer-oriented society

10. Many aspects of different cultural commons, especially their traditions of narratives and patterns of mutual support, carry forward prejudices and patterns of discrimination—thus the cultural commons should not be romanticized.

11. The world's diversity of cultural commons are being undermined (enclosed) by technological and market forces that are working to integrate them into the consumer culture.

12. Computer driven automation is also turning more aspects of the cultural commons into services and products that require

dependence upon the money economy that benefits the already wealthy at the further expense of the poor.

13. The teacher's role as a mediator is to help students articulate the differences in the development of personal talents, ecological footprint, and patterns of mutual support as they move between their cultural commons and market-based experiences.

14. One of the goals of the teacher's mediating role is to help students become more aware of the community's traditions of self-sufficiency and mutual support, and thus to be able to recognize when technologies and market forces threaten to overturn these traditions.

15. In helping students articulate these differences, as well as recognize aspects of the scientific and industrial culture that have made positive contributions to humankind, the teacher is addressing a fundamental problem in our increasingly complex democracy: namely, the ability on the part of the student to acquire the linguistic and conceptual basis for exercising communicative competence in the political process.

Ecology of Print-Based Storage and Computer-Mediated Learning:

1. Print-based cultural storage and thinking have radically different affects on consciousness and social relations—which are not understood by most public school teachers and university professors.

2. Print-based cultural storage and thinking have the following characteristics that are, in turn, influenced by differences in cultural ways of knowing:

    a. Print can only provide a surface understanding of ideas, events, and processes.

    b. Print is unable to represent the deep cultural and natural ecologies of information that underlie the origin and current influence of ideas, events, and processes that are inadequately represented by the word "context."

    c. What is committed to print becomes immediately outdated in a world of cultural and natural ecological systems that involve both historical continuities and constant change

    d.   Print reinforces abstract thinking and thus the tendency to treat abstract thinking as representing universals that no longer take account of different cultural and natural contexts.

    e.   Printed texts, whether in a book or on a computer screen, reinforce the conduit view of language that, in turn, hides the metaphorical and thus historical forces that continue to frame the meaning of many words.

    f.   One of the aspects of print that has a powerful influence on consciousness, and thus on social policies, is that print allows people who would otherwise be constrained by the misconceptions of their community to communicate their ideas to a broader and even a future audience.

3. Print too often is interpreted by the reader and even the writer as representing an objective account of reality.

4. Print reinforces key characteristics of modern western culture: the validity of the individual's perspective and critical analysis, sight as the source of knowledge, objective knowledge that can be universalized.

5. Printed accounts marginalize the information acquired through the senses other than sight, which print privileges.

6. Print has served as a key part of the process of colonization, in terms of maps that designate political boundaries without awareness of cultural differences of the groups within these boundaries, and the written treaties that do not take account of the cultural traditions of the groups constrained by the written treaties.

7. Literacy has served as justification for colonizing oral cultures that were seen as uncivilized and thus in need of being brought into the modern world which is largely dominated by abstract thinking and political ideologies.

8. Computer-mediated learning and thinking, as well as reliance upon other forms of Internet-based communication, reinforce the sense of being an autonomous individual and in control of where one wants to go in terms of cyberspace and thus the future.

9. Unlike oral cultures where elder wisdom and narratives carry forward the moral values and, in many instances, the knowledge

of how to live within the limits and possibilities of the local bioregion, computer and Internet based thinking marginalizes awareness that everything in the cultural and natural ecologies have a history—with implications for the prospects of an ecologically sustainable future.

10. One of the dominant influences of computer and Internet mediated thinking and communication upon consciousness is that cultural amnesia is becoming more widespread—which can also be understood as the loss of long-term memory.

11. Oral patterns of storage, thinking, and communication more often rely upon all the senses, and not just sight, and are more likely to avoid many of the limiting characteristics of print. Other implications include the following:

    a. Relying upon all the senses provides more access to the information being exchanged in the local cultural and natural ecologies.

    b. Oral communication increases awareness of ongoing relationships.

    c. Oral communication also relies more on active memory of the other participants in the relationship.

    d. Oral cultures are more community-centered which can lead to practices of mutual support, as well as discriminatory practice of members who are viewed as deviating from the shared moral norms. Tolerance of differences varies from culture to culture.

    e. Oral cultures vary in terms of their restrictions and allowances for participatory decision making, but they also have been more successful in the past of socializing the new generations to the moral norms governing human/nature relationships. This is now disappearing with the spread of literacy and the accompanying sense of individual autonomy.

    f. Oral cultures are coming under increasing pressure to adopt the print-based form of consciousness, which also includes adopting the western technologies that are alienating the youth of these cultures from the intergenerational traditions that underlie the cultural and natural commons.

Ecological Intelligence:

1. Scientists reduced the ancient Greek concept of "oikos" to the study and management of the natural environment, which subsequently became known as "ecology."

2. As Gregory Bateson points out, all systems, from the micro to the macro natural systems—and including cultural patterns of information exchange—are ecologies.

3. Just as there are ecologies of weeds, there are cultural ecologies based on misconceptions carried forward in the ecology of language.

4. One of these misconceptions that has led to important developments in the areas of civil liberties, but also to destructive developments in how the West has exploited the environment, is the idea that intelligence is an attribute of the autonomous individual.

5. Thinking of an individually-centered exercise of intelligence does not take account of how thinking, values, and behaviors are influenced by the metaphorical and thus historically influenced language acquired in becoming a member of the language community.

6. The key to understanding that all relationships within cultural and natural systems are a central feature of all living ecologies is the information that is in constant circulation within the ecology's subsystems—which may be at level of the genetic/electro-chemical exchanges that sustain biological systems and in the conversations between speakers. The responses that sustain life processes are triggered by what Bateson refers to as the "difference which makes a difference" in the response of the Other.

7. Human with human and human with nature relationships always, to varying degrees, take account of the differences communicated by the Other—which may be a change in the weather, the gesture or tone of voice of the Other, the off-key performance of other musicians, the use of words that have no relationship with other experienced realities, the introduction of a chemical that has a toxic effect on a biological system, and so forth.

8. Living in a world of ongoing and evolving relationships, where we are constantly aware and responding to differences (people walking on the wrong side of the street, the body language of the

Other, weather too extreme for the season, the absence of animal sounds, and so forth) means that everybody exercises in varying degrees ecological intelligence.

9. The exercise of ecological intelligence is not based on abstract thinking, but on the recognition that people are in varying degrees aware and respond to what is being communicated in their relationships within the cultural and natural ecological systems.

10. Playing a game, driving a car, cooking a meal, working with clay, interacting with students engaged in computer-mediated learning, and so forth, are the everyday examples of exercising ecological intelligence. There is always a question of whether awareness of relationships extends to those that are genuinely life-sustaining of the larger systems we are all dependent upon.

11. The misconceptions and silences encoded in the language influence which differences which make a difference that will be recognized and which ignored, and how the differences are interpreted. There is constant communication about the impact of the carbon footprint of Americans on natural systems—including the growing acidification of the world's oceans and the melting of the Artic ice—yet most Americans, while responding to other differences to which they have learned to observe and respond, continue to purchase vehicles that add to the carbon foot print.

12. The exercise of ecological intelligence should be understood as involving at least three different levels, though in some cultures the deep assumptions make the exercise of stage-three ecological intelligence a common feature of everyday life. What is noteworthy is that many of these cultures did not rely on western technologies that promote abstract thinking, the myth of individual autonomy and technologically driven progress that are now undermining these complex traditions of sustainable thinking and behavior.

13. The taken for granted cultural assumptions underlying the individual/consumer-dependent lifestyle promoted by the industrial culture leads to an individually-centered exercise of ecological intelligence. The information circulating through the relations is selectively perceived, and understood as part of strategy for achieving one's personal goals.

14. Stage-two ecological intelligence involves giving attention to the difference that make a difference—such as being aware of

inadequate diets among children, the way automation is displacing the need for workers, the efforts to suppress the ability of the poor and marginalized to vote in an election, and so forth. Taking this information into account leads to addressing social injustice issues.

15. Stage-three ecological intelligence involves awareness of social justice issues but also a concern with how to conserve as well as how to initiate changes that contribute to a sustainable future— for both the cultural and natural systems. Awareness that hyper-consumerism, and the language that provided conceptual direction to the Industrial Revolution that is now in its digital phase of globalization, are ecologically unsustainable would come naturally to a person who exercises stage-three ecological intelligence.

16. People who are more oriented to exercising sustainable ecological intelligence may at times operate at the level of individually-centered ecological intelligence, and even at the social justice level. In some cultures, stage two and three are a taken for granted ways of responding to the differences which make a difference in their lived ecologies.

17. A major obstacle to students becoming aware of the different stages of ecological intelligence is the modernizing ideology promoted in teacher education programs that go under different labels but share many of the same deep cultural assumptions of the market liberals who are promoting western assumptions and values as the basis of a new global economic order. These include critical pedagogy, transformative learning, place based education (which does not question the myth of individual intelligence), eco-pedagogy, and computer-mediated learning that reinforces abstract thinking and the idea that students should construct their own knowledge.

Implications that go beyond teacher education and curriculum classes:

Due to the time constraints of the summer class, as well as the pressure students were under from other classes, the exchanges indicated that some students were not doing all the readings, or were treating them too superficially. Nevertheless, most of the key ideas that brought a depth of understanding of the overall conceptual framework were briefly discussed, with many of the more important ones being examined in terms of how they lead to a more explicit awareness of how the curriculum, both spoken and written, reinforces the ecologically destructive patterns of thinking and values. There were also extended discussions of how key ideas lead to introducing curriculum changes at different levels in the educational process. A point that was stressed is that the curriculum reforms should enable students to understand that words have a history and encode earlier ways of thinking, that the cultural commons represent alternatives to a consumer-dependent lifestyle, that print-based storage (including Internet-based thinking and communication) undermines the exercise of ecological intelligence.

What is distinctive about making these language issues a central part of the teacher's professional knowledge, and which should be at the center of any university reform effort, is that the explanatory power of the key concepts listed above is not acquired by reading textbooks or downloading explanations from Google. Rather, the concepts help make explicit how the languaging processes in the curriculum reinforce the old patterns of thinking and limited awareness, or enable students to recognize patterns that before were hidden behind the fog of their taken for granted experience. That is, the emphasis was on how the concepts could be used to frame which aspects of the students otherwise taken for granted culture could be made explicit, described, and then examined in terms of its impact on their own lives, the affect on the well-being of the community and on natural systems. One of the key ideas in the above list is that reliance upon print-based descriptions leads to abstract thinking, and thus to a surface knowledge that does not take account of differences which make a difference within the local environmental and cultural ecologies.

The point was stressed over and over again that after introducing students to a brief introductory explanation that frames what the concept brings to awareness the focus should then shift to doing a deep-ethnography (similar to what Geertz referred to as a "thick description") of the patterns of behavior, thinking, and valuing that collectively constitute the living cultural and natural ecologies the students are embedded in. The teacher's role is that of a mediator who asks the questions, provides students the conceptual space to give words to what otherwise is part of their unrecognized and unarticulated taken for granted world, and at times reframes the issues in ways that help make explicit other processes and possible consequences the students may not have considered.

For example, asking students from different ethnic backgrounds to identify the analogs within their own culture that frame the meaning of words such as "tradition," "education," "sacred," "intelligence," "poverty," and so forth, and to compare these analogs with what most speakers of English take for granted can easily lead to a examination of how print serves to hide the cultural history of words—of both the dominant and ethnic cultures. After a careful and in-depth examination of the student's cultural commons, as well as what is shared across cultural groups, the teacher can ask students to do an in-depth ethnography of how the various Internet technologies that rely upon print and other abstract forms of representation affects awareness of the intergenerational communication that carries forward the cultural commons. The question that needs to be asked is how computer-mediated learning and participation in the many social networking systems contribute to undermining the cultural commons. This, in turn, will lead back to making explicit aspects of the students' culturally (that is, ethnically) mediated experience as well as to considering patterns they have observed within the larger society—to which they have not given serious thought.

The importance of relying upon the list of key concepts about the languaging processes that characterize all cultural ecologies is that they point to the need for students to learn about their own context-specific cultural patterns that affect their communities and the natural systems that are now being degraded. This is radically different from forcing students to acquire the abstract information that is framed by writers who are mostly unaware of the cultural assumptions that influence the interpretations they too often misrepresent as objective facts and information. The challenge is whether the current and future generations of students entering the teaching profession can recognize the misconceptions of their professors who are still under the influence of the conceptual orthodoxies of the late 20th century when there was little awareness of the cultural roots of the ecological crisis, and the ways in which print-based knowledge reproduce a surface knowledge of local contexts—as well as the silences in the thinking of the experts who produced it.

References

Bateson, G. 1972, *Steps to an Ecology of Mind*. New York: Ballantine Books.

_____. 1980. *Mind and Nature: A Necessary Unity*. New York. Ballantine Books

Bowers, C. 2005. *The False Promises of Constructivist Theories of Learning: A Global and Ecological Critique*. New York: Peter Lang.

_____. 2006 *Revitalizing the Commons: Cultural and Educational Sites of Resistance and Affirmation*. Lanham. Maryland. Lexington Books.

_____. 2011. *University Reform in an Era of Global Warming*. Eugene, OR. The Eco-Justice Press.

_____. 2011. *Perspectives on the Ideas of Gregory Bateson, Ecological Intelligence, and Educational Reforms*. Eugene, OR. The Eco-Justice Press.

_____. 2112, *The Way Forward: Educational Reforms that Address the Cultural Commons and the Linguistic Roots of the Ecological/ Cultural Crises*. Eugene, OR. The Eco-Justice Press.

Carr, N. 2011. *The Shallow: What the Internet is Doing to Our Brains*. New York: Norton.

Harries-Jones, P. 1995. *A Recursive Vision: Ecological Understanding and Gregory Bateson*. Toronto: University of Toronto Press.

Havelock, E. 1986. *The Muse Learns to Write: Reflections on Orality and Literacy from Antiquity to the Present*. New Haven, CT.: Yale University Press.

Ong, W. 1982. *Orality and Literacy: The Technologizing of the Word*. New York: Methuen.

Reddy, M. 1979, "The Conduit Metaphor—A Case of Frame Conflict in Our Language About Language." In *Metaphor and Thought*, edited by Andrew Ortony. Cambridge, G.B.: Cambridge University Press. 284-323.

Sachs, W. 1992. *The Development Dictionary: A Guide to Knowledge as Power*. London. Zed Books.

Shils, E. 1981. *Tradition*. Chicago: University of Chicago Press.

Chapter 4

Toward an Ecologically Informed Paradigm for Thinking About Educational Reforms

We are now at a turning point where the political language relied upon for promoting social justice and economic progress over the last five hundred years now prevents us from recognizing the cultural roots of the ecological crisis. The Classical Liberal theorists could not have anticipated that the economic forces their ideas unleashed would now become a major contributor to changing the chemistry of the world's oceans, to spreading toxic chemicals across the land, and to creating an individually centered lifestyle dependent upon consumerism. Nor could they anticipate a world population moving toward ten billion people who are faced with radically diminished resources. This chapter makes the case that the limitations of liberal thinking—its ethnocentrism to which is given only lip service, its failure to recognize that the ecological crisis is also a crisis in cultural ways of knowing, and its failure to recognize the deep cultural assumptions it shares with the market liberals and libertarians—should now give way to an ecological paradigm as the basis for thinking about educational reforms. The ecological paradigm informed by the thinking of Gregory Bateson avoids the ethnocentrism of both social justice and market liberals, human-centeredness, the myth of the individual's intellectual autonomy, and the authority of print-based abstract thinking. In their place, the ecological paradigm brings into focus interdependent relationships, how language carries forward the misconceptions of earlier eras, and an awareness that the diversity of the world's cultural commons represent alternatives to the environmentally destructive consumer culture that is now being globalized—ironically, in the name of progress.

The False Promises that Undermine a Sustainable Future

The use of words and phrases such as "individualism", "empowerment", "transformative learning", "critical pedagogy" and so forth, are intended to signal to readers that they are about to encounter the latest thinking of a liberal educational reformer. Unfortunately, this vocabulary, along with its underlying deep cultural assumptions that exclude other vocabularies better suited to clarifying the life-threatening challenges we now face, is still in the grip of centuries-old ways of thinking. Writing on the influences of liberalism on educational policies, practices, and discourse requires acknowledging that there are two traditions of liberalism: the liberalism focused on social justice issues and the neo or what I prefer to refer to as the market liberalism that is focused on economic globalization and maximizing profits for the few at the expense of the environment and the many. Both traditions of liberalism share many of the same deep cultural assumptions. The assumptions they share in common—that rational/critical thinking leads to a linear form of progress, that this is a human-centered world, that the individual is the basic social unit and source of intelligence, that traditions must be overturned in order to free the forces of innovation and individual emancipation, that technologies are both culturally neutral and the expression of progress, and that these assumptions should be the basis for promoting on a global scale the West's approach to social justice and economic development. That the latter is often in conflict with the former is ignored in the same way that the western thinkers who laid the conceptual basis for these assumptions also ignored their ethnocentric biases.

John Locke's epistemology marginalized the importance of traditional knowledge and established the conceptual basis for the ownership of private property (including as much as the individual could acquire). His ethnocentric and abstract thinking was matched by the ethnocentrism and abstract thinking of Adam Smith (who wrote the important yet neglected *A Preface to Moral Sentiments*), as well as the thinking of John Stuart Mill, and more recently John Dewey and Paulo Freire. They also shared other core assumptions that are still in vogue among both social justice and market liberals—assumptions that demonstrate how different genres of liberalism are still in the grip of a past that was unaware of environmental limits. Then and now references to the need for critical thinking to focus on what needs to be conserved as well as changed are still missing. What has become part of the litany of liberal educators is promoting the students' ability to engage in critical thinking in order to change the world—as if scientists, technocrats, and market liberal politicians are not changing the world fast enough. Critical thinking and transformative learning are now the mantra of the liberal educators guiding UNESCO's project of promoting sustainability thinking in teacher education programs around the world—which is yet another example of ethnocentric thinking. To fully understand this criticism, one needs to recognize the diverse cultural traditions that strengthen community, have a smaller ecological footprint, and have enabled people to live largely non-monetized lives.

One of the problems is that the word "liberalism" is a context-free metaphor. That is, it is the outcome of abstract thinking that has become disengaged from the historical experiences that shaped its earliest social justice priorities. Thus, Ayn Rand's idea that individuals should recognize and live by a rationally based ethic of selfishness and that capitalism represents the economic system that best allows a lifestyle of selfishness to be fully realized. Her brand of liberalism holds that altruism and government regulations undermine both the basic rights of the individual and social progress. She also promoted critical thinking as essential to recognizing how governmental efforts to provide a safety need for the disadvantaged is a violation of the individual's basic right to fail. Today's Tea Party activists are relying upon another liberal idea that has been widely promoted by educational reformers: namely, that individuals should construct their own knowledge and values. Scientific facts, knowledge that has been revised over generations of experience and varies from culture to culture, are to be ignored in favor of the individual's subjective decisions. Underlying the thinking of social justice liberals, market liberals, libertarians, Tea Party activists, and the followers of Dewey and Freire is that their various approaches to educational reforms are assumed to lead to social progress (which is another context-free metaphor).

Scientists are now claiming that the rate and scale of environmental change means that we may have only a few decades before we become overwhelmed by rising levels in the world's oceans, droughts and the increasing scarcity of potable water that will doom hundreds of millions to a level of poverty where life itself cannot be sustained, and the disappearance of species that rivals earlier mass extinctions. The majority of liberal educators seem not to recognize the connections between the deep cultural assumptions that underlie their interpretation of progress and how these assumptions guide policies and actions that are exacerbating the crisis—especially as these assumption are being embraced by other cultures that want to identify themselves as becoming modern and technologically developed.

The language of liberalism is like the early stages of a Tower of Babel discourse, with widely diverse groups using seemingly the same vocabulary of liberalism to achieve radically different social, economic, and colonizing agendas. What the followers of Classical Liberalism (Locke, Smith, Mill), of today's social justice liberals (Ayers, Dewey, Freire, Gadotti), and of the libertarian liberals (Rand, Norquist, the Republican alliance of Tea Party activists, corporate heads, and the military establishment) all ignore is that the ecological crisis has moved from being the focus of scientific research and publications to massively impacting people's daily lives. Fisheries are disappearing, droughts are spreading and jeopardizing the food security of entire nations, glaciers are melting at a rate that is threatening the prospects of billions of people. In the face of these immediate threats, it is necessary to ask whether there is an alternative paradigm that avoids the following: the ethnocentrism inherent in all genres of liberal thinking, the deep cultural assumptions derived from liberal thinking that underlie the industrial/consumer culture that is a major contributor to accelerating the rate of environmental change, and the Social Darwinian thinking that prevents many liberals from recognizing what can be learned from other cultures, including the traditions within our own dominant culture, that are more community rather than consumer and individualistic centered.

There are many indigenous cultures that have developed what can be referred to as ecological intelligence. That is, they learned by carefully observing the cycles of life-renewing processes within their bioregion, and this knowledge was then encoded in their languages. They also learned how to adapt their technologies and rituals in ways that did not destroy these ecological cycles of renewal. Of course, there are many indigenous cultures, as Jared Diamond points out in his book, *Collapse: How Societies Choose to Fail or Succeed* (2011) that failed to recognize how ecological uninformed practices and values were leading to their demise.

The important point here is that there is a small group of scientists and others who are beginning to understand the characteristics of ecologies in ways that take into account cultural practices and how even modern individuals exercise a limited form of ecological intelligence. The leading thinkers who are rescuing the concept of ecology from scientists who have traditionally understood it as the study of natural systems, which reflected a radically limited way of thinking, are now associated with the biosemiotic movement, and with the followers of the ideas of Gregory Bateson. For educators willing to move beyond the double bind thinking of Classical and contemporary interpretations of liberalism, and to explore the educational reform implications of Bateson's ecological interpretative framework, his insights on the role of language are especially critical. Chapter 2 of my recent book, *Perspectives on the Ideas of Gregory Bateson, Ecological Intelligence, and Educational Reforms* (published by the Eco-Justice Press, 2011) pulls together his ideas on language that are interspersed in various places in his *Steps to an Ecology of Mind* (1972), which many find difficult to understand because of their own taken for granted liberal/Enlightenment assumptions. Why Bateson rather than the writings of the biosemiotic thinkers should be the starting place for educational reformers is that Bateson's ideas help to clarify the how culture practices, including the role of language, need to be understood as ecologies. The emerging field of biosemiotics provides a way of understanding all natural systems, including cultural practices, as semiotic systems that are dependent upon the constant exchange at different levels and of kinds of information—chemical, temperature changes, genetic, silences, metaphorical, patterns of metacommunication between people, and so forth. But as biosemiotics is now dominated by scientists, the cultural/languaging processes so crucial to initiating substantive educational reforms are given less attention. I will reverse their orientation by presenting the characteristics of an ecological paradigm of understanding that avoids the ethnocentrism, Social Darwinian bias, and deep cultural assumptions that represent the individual as an autonomous, rational/critical thinker and the rest of the world, in Cartesian fashion. as unintelligent and as a non-participant in the dynamic nature of all living systems.

The cultural assumptions shared by different interpretations of the liberal agenda that were mentioned at the outset have no place in an ecological paradigm. But this paradigm provides a way of understanding how these assumptions continue to be perpetuated in the language of the classroom and in the media generally. It also brings into focus what the liberal myth of individual freedom has hidden: namely, that one of the most unique characteristic of all forms of life is that existence involves relationships. And this holds for the misleading metaphor we use to refer to the "individual," and the other misleading metaphor we associate the basic need of the individual for "freedom."

Bateson's famous saying that the "map is not the territory" is a key to understanding that there is no such entity as an autonomous individual, and that students and even the most creative thinkers do not construct their own ideas. Language as Bateson and others have pointed out, is metaphorical, and the analogs that frame the meaning of such words as "individual", "data", "intelligence", "woman", "progress", "technology", and so forth were settled upon in earlier times, and in cultural contexts, that led to these words now carrying forward the earlier ways of thinking—including misconceptions, silences, prejudices. When the infant begins learns to think and communicate in the metaphorical language of her/his linguistic community, the earlier patterns of thinking become taken for granted. Over time some of these earlier meanings are recognized as too constrictive and as sources of injustice, which then leads to adopting new analogs. This process of revising the meaning of words seldom involves revising the deep root metaphors such as progress, individualism, mechanism, anthropocentrism, economism, and so forth. The best example of how current interpretations of liberalism continues to perpetuate these deep root metaphors is that the word (metaphor) "tradition" still carries forward the failure of Enlightenment thinkers to recognize the traditions that sustained the skilled crafts of people and others who sustained the cultural commons of their day.

Ecologies, even ecologies of bad ideas or what Bateson refers to as ecologies of weeds, are sustained through various forms of communication. But unlike the liberal assumptions that represents individuals as rational actors in a non-intelligent world, Bateson claims that what circulates through all ecologies are differences which make a differences. The bosemiotic thinkers, such as Jesper Hoffmeyer and Wendy Wheeler, translate Bateson's famous saying into the language of semiotics and the emergent world of ongoing information exchanges. Bateson further argues that these difference are the basic units of information that lead to responses by the Other. The differences which make a difference, such as how toxic chemicals interact with the genetic codes regulating the development of the immune system, and as the teacher observes students texting messages (to cite just two examples), leads to communication that is interactive. The Other responds, which then becomes a difference that leads to further exchanges. For example, at the micro level of the ecologies within the human body, the receptors in cells respond to what is being communicated at the level of chemical/electrical processes. It is an interactive form of communication of information, and not a matter of thinking and acting on an inert world. Perhaps it is easier to recognize what Bateson means by a difference which makes a difference being the basic unit of information, and how it leads to interactive responses, by considering how a soccer player responds to the differences in the other players' behavior, which lead in turn to a dance in the interactions of the players. New ideas may also be the difference which makes a difference in thinking and behavior—or in the awareness that the use of genetically modified seeds that resist Roundup has an adverse impact on the environment which in turn is communicated through the growth of pesticide resistant super-size weeds. Everything in both natural and cultural ecologies communicate in response to differences which make a difference, and there are consequences that follow. But the misconceptions and silences encoded in the language of the culture may lead to the consequences that are life threatening to go unnoticed. That is, many of the differences which make difference in the viability of natural systems to support life are going unnoticed—which brings us to the question of how language inherited from the past continues to influences awareness.

The ecological paradigm of thinking leads to recognizing that what liberals represent as individual freedom should be more accurately understood as individuals **always** being in a relationship with the Other—another person or group, changes in the natural environment, the history of their own cultural ecology—including the ecology of its guiding languages, unjust and exploitive acts by others, behaviors that are mutually supportive, and so forth. Bateson's saying about maps (metaphorical language systems constituted in the past) not accurately representing the territory (today's problems and possibilities—including social injustices and ecologically unsustainable policies), also clarifies why the liberal view of individualism, including how individuals think about and use language, is also a product of abstract theory that has been repeated over the centuries. In order to maintain the myth that rational/critical thinking is free of cultural influences and thus of ethnocentrism, it is necessary, as Michael Reddy pointed out, to think of language as a conduit in a sender/receiver process of communication. This is the view of language reinforced at all levels of formal education, in the use of digital technologies, in the media, and in everyday conversations.

When Bateson's observation about the map/territory disconnect is related to what we now understand about the nature of metaphorical thinking, it becomes clearer that when supposedly autonomous thinkers engage in critical and transformative learning they are reproducing with only minor variations the conceptual maps of an earlier era when there was no understanding of environmental limits—and no understanding that not all cultures equate the hyper-rate of change with progress. An ecological perspective brings out that words, whether spoken or written, have a history, and that they are metaphors whose meaning were framed by the earlier selection of analogs that reflected the power relationships, misconceptions, and silences of earlier times. When a person is born into a language community, she/he learns to think in the metaphorical language inherited from the past. As we are witnessing, some of these earlier analogs are being revised—such a how thinking of a woman as an artist and mathematician (exluded possibilities in terms of earlier analogs), that wilderness is a sign of a healthy ecosystem (rather than wild and needing to be brought under technological control).

What is being suggested here is that in recognizing that most of the language of liberalism (how traditions, individuals, intelligence, language, technology, and so forth are understood) is metaphorical and still carries forward the misconceptions and silences of earlier thinkers who did not recognize how relying upon print promotes abstract thinking that is ethnocentric and that undermines the exercise of ecological intelligence, we can then recognize important reforms that must be undertaken in the area of curriculum. The cultural assumptions identified earlier as being shared by different interpretations of liberalism—such as an anthropocentric world, individualism, progress, mechanism, economism, and so forth—are also root metaphors that influence thought and behavior across a wide range of cultural activity, and over hundreds of years. Some root metaphors are being challenged, such as patriarchy, while new ones are beginning to provide different ways of understanding, such as evolution (which supports the assumptions of the market liberals) and ecology (which helps us understand how mechanistic science can lead to misconceptions that threaten life itself). As evidence of the influence of root metaphors we have only to consider the role of Social Darwinian thinking in the shaping the internal and foreign policies of Nazi Germany. Two more observations need to be made about the role of root metaphors: as powerful interpretative frameworks they control which vocabularies are conceptually coherent while at the same time marginalizing other vocabularies. They also operate below the level of conscious awareness, which is further aided by thinking of language as a conduit in a sender/receiver process of communication.

The metaphorical nature of words illuminate and hide. Root metaphors do the same thing but operate on a scale that has global consequences—which we can now witness in the globalization of the market liberal agenda. What is hidden by the language-controlling root metaphors underlying the industrial culture are the changes occurring in the natural system.

Educational Reforms that Address Social and Eco-Justice within an Ecological Paradigm

What are the pedagogical and curricular reforms that will help the younger generations avoid the conceptual grip of classical and current social justice and market liberal ideologues? The initial reaction to the curriculum reforms suggested at the end of the last chapter may lead teachers to claim that their professional courses did not prepare them to introduce students to an in-depth examination of the cultural patterns in their own cultural ecologies. They may also protest that there are no written texts on how to proceed. What needs to be understood is that a curriculum that focuses on the lived cultural ecologies of the students should not be derived from printed accounts, either in textbooks or on a computer screen. Rather it can be described by students if the teacher asks them the right questions that will being to their attention patterns of communication and behavior that were previously taken for granted. The teachers' task is to name the patterns, and then engage students in the process of examining how the patterns affect other patterns, relationships, and long-term consequences.

What students will be learning is the key characteristics of ecological thinking: that is, learning to give explicit attention to what is being communicated in their relationships, both natural and cultural, that are that part of the embodied experiences. They will also be learning that the ecological conceptual framework is not ethnocentric, nor does it lead to a human-centered way of thinking and acting in the world. As students become aware of the metaphorical language of their own culture (including its history), and the differences that make a difference when foreign metaphors are introduced, they will then be able to recognize how the languaging processes that are taken for granted hide and illuminate changes occurring in the ecological systems they depend upon. As suggested earlier, naming the patterns that are part of the students' everyday experiences should be the starting place for in-depth discussions. From time to time the teacher may need to explain how the patterns connect and interact on each other.

Summary:

If the above analysis were to be boiled down the most essential points it would be that liberalism, for all the gains made in moving us beyond the constraints of feudalism and early capitalism, carries forward too many of the assumptions that have contributed to the industrial culture that is now accelerating the degradation of the natural environment. The conceptual roots of liberalism are in print-based abstract thinking that failed in the past, and continues to fail today, in recognizing the cultural roots of the ecological crisis, and that different cultures have taken other routes to development that have had a smaller adverse environmental impact. Bateson and other thinkers have laid the groundwork for recognizing that all ecological systems, both natural and cultural, possess the observable characteristics that suggest the nature of educational reforms that must be undertaken. Engaging students in deep ethnographies of their own cultural patterns will enable them to make explicit the ecologically destructive patterns that they will otherwise continue to take for granted unless patterns and relationships are made explicit and examined in terms their environmentally destructive consequences, and their other life-enhancing possibilities.

Chapter 5

One of the Political Legacies of Print-Dominated Thinking: Ayn Rand's Justification of the Pursuit of a Life of Selfishness

One would think that the thousands of deaths and misuse of the national wealth resulting from foreign wars justified on the grounds of spreading "freedom," "democracy," and "modernization," would make people wary of the abstract language of politicians. Yet one of the most pervasive characteristics of today's political discourse, particularly among Republicans and their extremist political base, is the use of context-free metaphors and phrases that do not connect with the diverse cultural realities of people's lives. These metaphors—"freedom," "religion," "progress," free-markets," "limited government," "national security," "individualism," "terrorism," "liberalism," and so forth, are politically important in ways not understood by the politicians and members of the general public who use them. Unfortunately, the ritualistic and obfuscating functions of these context-free metaphors too often represent a reality to which people must submit. There are many reasons that formal education have left most people unable to recognize the dangers of basing political decisions on abstractions that preclude any possibility of being held accountable for facts, evidence, and the failure of social policies based on previous abstract thinking.

As the current debates about the future of the country grind on, it is evident that abstract ideas continue to energize people in ways that diminish their ability to think critically about whether the abstract ideas actually take account of the on-the-ground realities that are inescapable aspects of people's lives. Perhaps if their public school and university education had introduced them to the fundamental differences between oral and print-based thinking and communication, as discussed in the writings of Walter Ong, Eric Havelock, and Jack Goody, they would have the conceptual basis necessary for recognizing the connections between how print-based storage and thinking leads only to surface knowledge that quickly becomes outdated and thus a misrepresentation of the ongoing flow of daily life. As students they might have also learned to recognize how the printed word marginalizes awareness of local contexts and tacit understandings—and even more important, how the printed word always represents the writer's culturally influenced interpretative framework and, to borrow a phrase from Friedrich Nietzsche, the deep and generally hidden psychological forces that drive the writer's will to power. It is a myth that there can be an objective account of events, ideas, and data that does not involve someone's observations and interpretations, or a machine-based approach to obtaining evidence that does no involve the biases of the people who designed the machine. Print is only one of a culture's multiple uses of language that sustain what its members take to be reality. It also needs to be remembered that print and the spoken abstractions that result from the over-emphasis of print-based knowledge in the West also represent a particular cultural way of knowing and a particular stage in the development of the culture. Contrary to the thinking of many people, abstract words such as "freedom," "free-markets," "democracy," and so forth, do not refer to universal values or practices, but are culturally specific. Earlier examples of the political power of abstract words such as "primitive," 'New World," and "Manifest Destiny" also reflected culturally-based misconceptions that were successfully used for colonizing purposes.

The West has a long history of privileging print-based accounts of reality over the face-to face relationships valued within different cultures. For example, we have only to recall the abstract theories of western philosophers, from Plato to Dewey, as well as other theorists in the fields of economics, psychology, and education to see how the tacitly understood and practiced daily cultural patterns, beliefs, and practices have been ignored. The mid-20th century thinking of Ayn Rand that now exerts such a powerful influence on today's political discourse simply continues the long history of privileging abstract thinking and theory over ways of thinking that take account of local cultural contexts. This tradition of thinking, which Ayn Rand now models for the current leaders of the Republican Party and its political base, and is still carried on in most areas of the public school and university curricula, continues the age-old silences in the West about the cultural roots of the ecological crisis. This crisis includes how oceans are undergoing chemical changes that threaten the basis of the food chain, global warming that is melting glaciers and thus threatening the sources of fresh water for billions of people, and the continued genetic disruptions within plants, animals, and humans introduced in the name of progress (another context-free metaphor) by generations of scientists who only recently have learned to think of natural systems as ecologies. That all aspects of culture, from interpersonal interactions to the languaging processes that sustain people's taken for granted world, are also ecologies is still not understood by most scientists who continue to promote the agenda of the industrial/ consumer dependent culture.

In order to recognize the parallels between Ayn Rand's core ideas and the political agenda now being articulated by the leaders of the Republican Party and taken for granted by the Republican base, it is necessary to summarize the nature of the Objectivist ethic which she explains in *The Virtue of Selfishness* (1961). The lead chapter was the basis of the paper she presented at the University of Wisconsin Symposium on "Ethics in Our Times." It also summarizes the values and ideas that motivated the main characters in her widely read novels *The Fountainhead* (1943) and *Atlas Shrugged* (1957)—two books that had sold 25 million copies by 2007, and an additional 800,000 copies in 2008. She rejected both the labels of libertarianism and conservatism, but instead referred to her ideas as Objectivism. Nevertheless, her ideas are now considered foundational to the proponents of libertarianism and what has become mislabeled as conservatism. Indeed, her ideas are the basis of the Tea Party Movement, the economic policies promoted by Alan Greenspan, the rank and file Republican members of Congress, the majority of the Supreme Court, and the mix of political groups that make up the extreme right—including the right-wing media.

The widespread adoption of Rand's core ideas by libertarian and faux conservatives who have the support of a large segment of the American public is accelerating the polarization of American politics, and moving the country closer to what the German political theorist, Carl Schmitt, referred to as "friend/enemy" politics that precludes compromising with the enemy. In the following overview of Rand's core ideas of Objectivism, it is important to keep in mind that the focus is on how her language, and the language of her contemporary political followers, reflect a reliance upon abstractions that do not take account of the complex cultural and natural ecologies within which people live. To make this point in another way, the abstract thinking of Rand and her many followers represents a pseudo-reality, as it is not informed by the differences in cultural ecologies that characterize people's daily experience. And this pseudo-reality, like other print-based representations of reality such as the patriarchal God of the printed Bible, have become a source of personal motivation that fails to recognize the contradictions between the abstract ideas and values and the everyday world of interdependencies that cannot be accounted for by the abstract language. The denial on the part of the person who takes for granted the existence of public services such as the police, the fire and police protection, roads, schools, and the enforcement of public safety standards, while steadfastly claiming that all aspects of life should be regulated by the free-enterprise system, is a typical example of the political schizophrenia that can in part be attributed to the willingness to follow the leadership of abstract thinkers, politicians, and media demagogues.

Rand's theory of Objectivism relies upon the same tradition of abstract thinking found in the writing of the major western philosophers ranging from Plato, Locke, Descartes, and Hegel, to such contemporary theorists as John Dewey and Richard Rorty. And like these earlier abstract theorists, she fails to consider the following questions: Does Rand consider the differences in cultural ways of knowing, and how these differences are ignored when relying upon abstract representations of reality that provide only surface information? Do her abstract explanations of the ideas and values that should guide an individual's life take account of the interdependencies as well as the shaping influences of being born into a culture, as well as the individual's dependency on natural systems that are the sources of protein, water, oxygen, shelter, and the security that comes from not knowing that these natural systems are now on the verge of collapse? Do her abstractions accurately represent the life-sustaining and enhancing, as well as the life-destructive, characteristics of the local cultural commons? Is *The Virtue of Selfishness* a guidebook on anti-democratic thinking? These questions bring into focus a fundamental fact of life: namely, that her abstractions misrepresent the complexity of how an individual's life is influenced by the cultural and natural ecologies into which she/he is born. More importantly, her silences on how her abstract representations of how life should be lived, as well as the role of economic and governmental policies that are consistent with her abstract representation of a rationally based Objectivist ethic have not become a concern to the followers of her ideas.

The title of her guide to how to live by the Objectivist ethic, *The Virtue of Selfishness*, can easily lead to misunderstandings, which she recognized. Thus, she states in the Introduction that the word selfishness refers to prioritizing the "concern with one's own interests." (vii) Selfishness is not to be associated with greed, a nihilistic pursuit of self interest, and behaviors motivated by naivety or romantic thinking. As she put it: "The Objectivist ethics holds that the actor must always be the beneficiary of his actions and that man must act for his own *rational* self-interest." (x) The rational pursuit of self-interest, in turn, is justified on the grounds that the individual's primary goal is to sustain her/his life. That which threatens the life of the individual is evil, while what furthers her/his life is the good.

In order to understand Rand's other key ideas that relate to the role of the economic system, the legitimate role of government, and the rights of the individual, it is necessary to summarize the other values upheld by the Objectivist ethic. She identifies the three "values, which together, are the means to and the realization of one's ultimate value, one's own life—(which) are: Reason, Purpose, Self-Esteem, with their three corresponding virtues: Rationality, Productiveness, Pride." (25) To understand the full implications of what she means by these three metaphors, it is important to avoid summaries that fall short of how she explains the responsibilities of the individual—if her/his rationality is to sustain a life of freedom. Living a life based on Rationality, she writes, "means the recognition and acceptance of reason as one's *only* source of knowledge, one's *only* judge of value and one's *only* guide to action. It means one's total commitment to a state of full, conscious awareness, to the maintenance of a full mental focus in all issues, in all choices, in all of one's waking hours. It means a commitment to the fullest perception of reality within one's power." (25, italics added)

Her understanding of the individual's productiveness also eliminates the tendency of individuals to claim that their lives have been limited by outside influences, such as the existence of technologies that reduce the need for workers or being born into an impoverished family that failed to instill the Objectivist ethic and thus the rational basis necessary for a life of self-direction and freedom. "The virtue of Productiveness," she writes, "is the recognition of the fact that productive work is the process by which man's mind sustains his life, the process that sets man free of the necessity to adjust himself to his background, as all animals do, and gives him the power to adjust his background to himself. Productive work," she continues, "is the road to man's unlimited achievement and calls upon the highest attributes of his character" which she lists as "his refusal to bear uncontested disasters and his dedication to the goal of reshaping the earth in the image of his values." (26)

The virtue of Pride further limits the possibility of making excuses for personal failings and for placing the blame on outside forces. As she put it in *Atlas Shrugged,* "as man must produce the physical values he needs to sustain his life, so he must acquire the values of character that make his life worth sustaining—that as man is a being of self-made wealth, so he is a being of self-made soul." (27) And finally, the Objectivist ethic requires that "to live for his own sake means that the highest achievement of his own happiness is man's highest moral purpose." (27)

A key part of her theory, which now has become a central tenet of her followers, is that the life of the free and rational individual can only be achieved in a society where "pure" and unregulated capitalism exists. In order to attain the state of pure capitalism, she identifies another set of values and behaviors that a man of selfishness must meet. Again, she does not derive her list from a democratic process or a study of different cultural ways of understanding the moral values governing people's economic relationships. Rather, she reproduces from her study of Plato and other western philosophers at Petrograd State University in the Bolshevik transformed Russia the same pattern of abstract thinking that she expects "men" to accept as guides for living their rationally directed lives. Again it is important to give close attention to her exact words as they have become an important influence on current thinking and policy objectives of the Republicans who are, and it's not entirely clear here, either leading or following the libertarian, market-liberal voters. The principles guiding her view of economic man, which she identifies as a "trader" are equally straight forward and free of any complexities that most people encounter in everyday experience. As Rand puts it, "*The trader is a man who earns what he gets and does not give or take from the undeserved.* He does not treat men as masters or as slaves, but as independent equals.... *He does not switch to others the burden of his failures, and he does not mortgage his life into bondage to the failure of others."* (31, italic added) This statement, more than any other, summarizes how most Republicans now justify the limited role of government in addressing social justice issues.

Rand makes no suggestions for how people are to be held accountable when they stray from the Darwinian implications implicit in the Objectivist ethic, such as Warren Buffett's suggestion that the super-rich should pay more in taxes than what their secretaries pay. Indeed, her abstract theory for organizing society and defining the nature of moral relations does not include a discussion of how people are to be held accountable when they exploit others, such as we now see in the new CEO of Apple Computer being paid $378 million in his first year on the job. (R. Lowenstein, 2012) For Rand, there is no moral issue in the disparity between the salary of the Apple CEO and the economic and physical exploitation of the workers in China who assemble the Apple products. Not only is the CEO of Apple an "independent equal" of the Chinese assembly line workers, but according to Rand the government has no right to intrude into the relationship by taxing the Apple CEO as a way of redistributing wealth to the more vulnerable individuals. Again, her no-compromise position on the possibility that social justice issues should be addressed by government can be seen in what she claims to be the only proper role of government—a view that is now shared by the anti-government Republicans who also want to return to the Founding Fathers' Constitution—which in their day did not include an awareness of the need for government to regulate corporate abuses.

"The only proper, *moral* purpose of government is to protect man's rights, which means: to protect him from physical violence—to protect his right to his own life, to his own liberty, to his own *property* and to the pursuit of his own happiness. Without property rights, no other rights are possible. (33) That is, the government has no right to penalize the strong in order to reward or help the weak—a practice that current GOP presidential candidates view as leading Americans down the slippery slope of what they view as European totalitarian socialism. Rand's core ideas are in agreement with the libertarian CATO Institute's three-fold understanding of the role of government, as well as that of the other market-liberal think tanks such as the American Enterprise and Hoover Institutes. These mislabeled conservative think-tanks all claim that governments should be limited to promoting free-enterprise, individualism, and a strong national defense.

Rand's ideas have clearly influenced the ideas of Ron Paul as well as the majority of the Republican members of Congress—as well as the public that voted them into office. While her ideas are stated in a categorical way that does not allow for compromise and extenuating circumstances, the current direction in which the Republicans and their populist base of support are attempting to move the country reflects an effort to achieve the fullest realization of her abstract ideas—which includes the following:

(1) **On the universality of her Objectivist ethic**: Rand represents the rational capacity of "man" to live in accordance with the Objectivist ethic to be a universal of the human condition and thus unaffected by cultural differences. This leads, in turn, to legitimizing the right of the governmental and churches, and any other group that has a colonizing agenda, to promote American exceptionalism as the standard that other cultures are expected to emulate. Thus, when armed groups react to America's colonizing agenda, they must be attacked as a threat to national security. This leads, in turn, to a constant state of war that benefits both the military and the corporations. The Objectivist view of "man's" universal quest to place his/her survival interest above all other values, including what Rand regards as the misguided and degenerate nature of altruistic values, means that the loss of the diversity of the world's culture, as well as their language systems, represent the further elimination of old systems of beliefs that are not based on the Objectivist's individually-centered rationalism.

(2) **The Objectivist way of thinking about the role of education in perpetuating the freedom and survivability of the individual**: Rand and her Republican followers view public education as imposing the beliefs and practices of the larger hedonistic society, thus making it difficult for individuals to realize their own rational capacity for self-direction. The problem is that most parents have been indoctrinated by teachers who promote the common good over the pursuit of self-interest. The result is that parents are too willing, according to

most Republicans, to surrender their responsibility for guiding their children in how to live in accordance with the principles of Objectivism. The parents' proper role is to home-school their children, or to become supporters of charter schools whose guiding ideology can be more easily controlled by like-minded people.

(3) **Rand's view of property:** Rand's understanding of the role of government is that it is to be severely limited, especially as it relates to taxing what people have earned. Her thinking is clearly represented in Grover Norquist's alliance with corporations and other powerful opponents of taxes. Again, her abstract and categorical way of thinking fails to consider how the infrastructure and public services ranging from police, fire protection, and road and bridge maintenance, which both individual citizens and businesses rely upon, need to be paid for by the people who use them. To recall her views on the moral purpose of government: "it is to protect man's rights, which means to protect him from physical violence—to protect his right to his own life, to his own liberty, to his own property and to his own happiness." Only then will rationally-directed men realize the fullest potential of laissez-faire capitalism. (33) The majority of members on the Supreme Court as well as Congressional Republicans agree with Rand that capitalism "is the system of the future—if mankind is to have a future." Rand's universalism supports another agenda of Republicans, as well as most Democrats who acquired the same assumption from their university education: namely, that capitalism should be globalized—even if it requires the exercise of military force.

(4) **Rand's view of a life guided by reason:** She is explicit that this requires ignoring the opinions and evidence presented by others, especially those working for the state. She further claims that this is a preconditions of men becoming "dedicated to the goal of reshaping the earth in the image of [their] values." (26) Rand was writing at a time when few scientists were aware of the extent of the ecological crisis, and were, instead, unknowingly following her injunction that the environment should be shaped in terms of human values. The introduction of life-altering synthetic chemicals was viewed by the majority in the scientific

community as bringing the environment under rational control. Among the majority of professors in the social sciences and humanities, as well as in professional schools, the cultural assumptions that were undermining the life-sustaining natural ecologies were largely ignored—which largely persist today. Over the last 50 years there has been a radical shift in the scientific understanding of the changes occurring in natural systems, with the consensus research findings being reported in both scientific journals as well as in the public media not controlled by the major corporations. In spite of the scientific reports and visual evidence that now has become part of people's experience (such as increasing shortages of potable water, droughts, dying off of forests on a Biblical scale, changes in the growing seasons due to global warming, and the rapid decline in the world's fisheries, and so forth) the Republicans continue to view the environment as an exploitable resource. For them (and for Rand), this means the exploitation of the environment should be under the control of the free-market system. It also means that the Environmental Protection Agency must be eliminated—along with all the environmental regulations supported by Republicans during the presidency of Richard Nixon.

As pointed out earlier, the privileging of print-based storage and thinking (that is, abstract thinking) did not originate with Rand. Indeed, its roots go back much further in the history of the West when the printing press and the spread of literacy began to marginalize the importance of face-to-face communication, along with personal memory and the physical senses that are more attuned to acquiring a deeper understanding of local contexts and tacit understandings. Indeed, one can make the case that the oral traditions of the early Judeo/Christian world were transformed when they were reproduced as printed texts by men who represented different cultural ways of knowing. It is also worth considering that the certainties that many people associate with the printed word and the increased pressure on Republican politicians to adopt even more extreme abstract policies can be traced to the powerful consciousness shaping experience of relying upon how the printed word in the Bible creates a sense of reading universal truths and the actual words of God.

As students move from the elementary grades through the advanced stages of formal education, a greater emphasis is places on the authority of the printed word, and on even more abstract symbol systems. What can be more abstract than the numbers that underlie statistics—or "objective data"? With recent innovations in digital technologies there has been a slight recovery of visual and auditory representations of reality. Nevertheless, the complexity of local contexts, which include the ongoing micro and macro changes in both the cultural and natural ecologies, are largely sacrificed in achieving the supposed efficiencies and certainties of abstract thinking. The point to be made in understanding Rand's influence is that her own education, as it did for most authors and nearly all academics and public school teachers who unconsciously reproduce the taken for granted patterns of thinking of their mentors, was guided by deeply and widely held assumptions of the elites who established the abstract nature of high status knowledge— which meant treating knowledge obtained in face-to-face relationships as having low-status. Ironically, the basis of her unyielding commitment to a life guided by the rationality of the autonomous individual can be located in culturally-specific historical processes and assumptions of which she was unaware.

Other Myths and Silences in the Thinking of Ayn Rand, and People Whose Lives and Politics are Based on Similar Abstractions:

In order to avoid relying upon another either/or cultural pattern of thinking, which perpetuates its own reductionism, it must be stated that print is not the problem. Rather, it is how it is used. That is, print is highly useful when informed by the actual evidence of events, the complexities and contexts that influence people's ideas and behaviors, and an effort to bring to the attention of the reader the inherent limitations of what is represented in print. The latter, as both Walter Ong and Jack Goody have pointed out, is that what appears in print cannot replicate the ongoing flow of experience. Once in print, the reality it represents is fixed. Readers then bring their largely taken for granted interpretative frameworks to the printed text, which too often reduces further the accuracy of the printed word. This pattern can easily be seen in how commentaries on a book fails to take account of further changes in the author's ideas. The other inherent characteristic of print, which has been mentioned earlier, is that it cannot fully reproduce the complexity of local contexts, inner states of mind, tacit understandings, and what both the author and the people take for granted. To reiterate, print is a powerful and highly useful when its limitations are understood. The problem is that the various educational processes in western cultures fail to clarify its inherent limitations, and when it is being used in ways that are highly useful. To reiterate another point: Ayn Rand and the people who share many of her ideas about individual autonomy, the rational process, and how government must not interfere with the free markets, fail to understand how relying upon abstract metaphors leads to policies that are exacerbating the plight of millions of people through no fault of their own, and are further undermining the life-sustaining capacity of natural systems. The social justice issues that are marginalized by the abstract vocabulary of the Republicans and other right-wing groups will soon lead to levels of desperation where people will take to the streets in protest. This will lead to the full apparatus of a police state being relied upon by those who are using government and the media to further their own political and economic interests.

The focus from here on will be on the misconceptions that underlie Rand's key metaphors of "rationality," "individualism," "free markets," "altruism," and "limited government,"—as well as what she and her Republican and right-wing populist fellow-travelers ignore.

(1) **Rationality**: Rand's thinking about the power of rational thought to lead to a life of individual autonomy centered upon self-interest fails to take account of the influence of language on how rationality is understood and exercised. As Rand demonstrates, her supposedly culturally uninfluenced explanations about the nature and role of rationality are dependent upon the use of words—words that are metaphors that have a cultural history in terms of carrying forward the analogs that frame the meaning of the words (metaphors) she takes for granted. What Gregory Bateson refers to as the "recursive epistemologies" and which I call root metaphors, are the tacit background culturally derived conceptual frameworks that Rand relies upon in making the argument that the individual's rationality should determine what contributes to the *"maintenance of the organism's life."* In short, the root metaphors that are part of the ecology of language she takes for granted, and which are fundamental to her misunderstanding of a rational process that is free of

cultural influences, include the root metaphors of patriarchy, individualism, progress, anthropocentrism, economism, and a Social Darwinist spin on evolution. Her misconceptions about the nature of the rational process can be traced to her lack of awareness of how language carries forward many of the misconceptions and silences of earlier western thinkers, as well as their hubris.

(2) **Individualism**: Rand's views on the autonomy of individual thought, where she urges the individual to live "by the work of one's own mind," and to never place any value or consideration whatsoever above one's perception of reality," reflects another widely held myth in the West. Namely, that there is such a thing as an autonomous individual who is free of all outside influences. Indeed, this myth is still the basis of thinking of many educators who urge students to construct their own ideas. Even Paulo Freire argued that individuals can only achieve their fullest human potential as they question the thinking and achievements of previous generations, and rename the world for themselves.

A point that Gregory Bateson makes is that individuals cannot understand themselves, nor be understood by others, without taking into consideration their relationships within the cultural and natural ecologies. That is, all forms of life from the micro level of genes to the macro level of cultural and global natural systems exist in relationships. Without these relationships, which are also sources of interdependencies, the individual would cease to exist. If the individual's relationship with other members of the language community she/he is born into did not exist, the individual would be unable to think, be understood by others, or have a self-identity. And if the ecosystems collapse, which Rand urges being exploited by individuals who are to pursue their own self-interest and who are to promote a totally unrestrained capitalism, the individual would die of starvation. It's important to note how Rand viewed as a liberal hoax the scientific warnings about smoking, yet died of lung cancer—after using the name of Ann O'Connor in order to have her treatment paid for by Medicare. Today, her followers, as well as people who derived their anti-science thinking from other sources, promote the idea that all governmental restraints on exploiting the earth's natural resources should be eliminated. Individualism and pure, unrestrained capitalism are necessary "if humankind is to have a future," as she put it. (33)

(3) **Altruism**: According to Rand, the values and behaviors associated with altruism are sources of deception and a strategy for undermining the rational self-direction of the individual. "Today," she wrote, "the world is facing a choice: if civilization is to survive, it is the altruistic morality that men have to reject." All acts intended to help others, according to Rand's rationalistic ethic of selfishness, are really intended to take control of other people's lives. The moral ethic that is in accord with pure, unregulated capitalism is the ethic of selfishness; that is, relying upon one's own rational capacity for self-direction. Like Rand's other context-free metaphors, she does not consider the various cultural contexts in which altruism plays an important role in improving the quality of daily life that otherwise may become nasty, brutish, and short—to recall Thomas Hobbe's observation that applies to a world where caring for the well-being of others is absent.

It is important to note yet another convergence between the ideas of Rand and those held by Republicans in Congress and their populist right-wing base. That is, they view taxing the successful in order to provide a safety net for the unemployed, medically destitute, and people who started life below the poverty line, as a form of theft—and if any government assistance is to be given it must be paid for by reducing other governmental services. Acts of altruism are thus not consistent with the political economy of the market system, which the already rich control through their army of lobbyists

It's particularly interesting that many Christians who supposedly are committed to the Social Gospel of the New Testament, and thus to the tradition of helping those in need, are among the loudest supporters of the Republicans who want to use government to further advance the interests of the already wealthy. Just as in the examples of Rand's abstract understanding of rationality, individualism, and altruism, she ignores that these metaphors have different meanings in other cultures, and when related to local contexts, referred to earlier as the cultural and natural ecologies, they take on a complexity that is hidden when they are represented in print. To reiterate a point made earlier, the printed word provides only a surface and thus abstract knowledge that allows the writer to hide her/his ignorance of the tacit and contextual nature of everyday life.

(4) **Limited Government**: This is a mantra in both the thinking of Rand as well as today's Republican politicians and their populist base of supporters. Promoting the idea that government has to be limited to what the framers of the Constitution had in mind, which in their time did not include an awareness that the logic of capitalism requires the incessant drive to increase profits by exploiting workers, consumers, and the natural environment, serves to hide a dominant aspect of capitalism that Rand ignores. Without governmental regulation we would still have the exploitation of child labor, and workers in general. Women and other marginalized groups would still be subjected, without legal recourse, to the prejudices of the employer. Companies would be free to sell products without regard for health and other safety issues. This idea of shrinking government, which goes deeper in the history of the West than the current efforts of Grover Norquist and his corporate supporters, is rooted in the internal logic of a capitalistic economic system. But what Rand's defense of capitalism fails to recognize is that unregulated capitalism will ensure that the earth's natural systems become so degraded that humans and other species will not have a future.

This logic has now reached the point where the drive to reduce the cost of production in order to increase profits leads to adopting labor saving technologies that, in turn, lead to massive unemployment and thus to a reduction in the ability of people to consume on the scale required by the industrial system. This leads to the spiral downward we are now witnessing where the threat of reduced profits leads to the further automation of the production process, which leads to the further reduction in the need for workers. The massive unemployment, which in some countries is nearly 50 percent, is leading to levels of social chaos that, in turn, threaten to overthrow the governments—which then leads to the use of police and the army to suppress the unrest.

The Republicans and their populist and right-wing supporters seem unable to recognize the global scale of unrest resulting, in part, from the way in which the digital phase of the industrial revolution is making workers redundant, and how the current tax policies of the American government support this downward spiral into social chaos. On the other hand, the leadership, which draws support from corporations, the military and surveillance agencies, and the leadership of religious fundamentalists who want more influence in government in exchange for their support, may have recognized that democracy is the problem, and that policies that increase social unrest provide the opportunity to follow the Chinese model of a capitalist economy that operates under the centralized control of the state. Whatever frees capitalism from government regulation and the threats from street protesters would meet with the approval of Rand.

The Role of Public School and Universities in Promoting Print-Based Abstract Thinking:

There are many ways in which the patterns of thinking and communication become abstract and thus disconnected from the contexts of lived experiences that are best exemplified in the immediacy of face-to-face exchanges and patterns of mutual support. The spoken word, when passed from person to person, and over many generations, also becomes increasingly abstracted from the original event and from cultural/environmental ecologies in which the event occurred. The spoken exchanges quickly lose accuracy in terms of accounting for all the tacit and culturally implicit messages exchanged in face-to-face interactions. As the spoken word is retold by others there is a progressive loss of information which Bateson refers to as the differences which make a difference in human and nature relationships. Over time, the spoken word may also become a source of abstract thinking and communication. As the spoken word is repeated by others who are unaware of the original context, there is a greater likelihood that the taken for granted interpretative frameworks of the speakers and listeners will further distort how the original events occurred. The key point is that the spoken word, which includes narratives and the ceremonies they are based upon, can also become as divorced from the complexities of experience and events as is the case with the printed word.

However, there is a basic difference in the power relationship between speakers and writers, and thus between the listener and the reader. In terms of spoken relationships, there is a greater possibility of a shared background of cultural memory, as well as history of personal relationships—which may lead to an awareness that the speaker has a history of dishonesty, or being unable to remember accurately. Awareness of class, gender, and ethnic differences may lead to a more questioning attitude. In short, in terms of the immediate context of speaking and listening, which may move to the level of dialogue, there is often the possibility of questioning the speaker in ways that hold her/him to be accountable for what is spoken. In effect, spoken exchanges involve a different power relationship than is present in the relationship between the writer and the reader. To stay with Rand's relationship to her readers, the power relationship is asymmetrical. There is no possibility of an ongoing exchange between the reader and the development of the abstract arguments she commits to print. Thus, there is no way to challenge her ideas, and thus no immediate way to hold her accountable for basic misconception and silences. Nor can suggestions be made about where she might strengthen her arguments before she writes them down.

While memory and personal judgments enter into oral exchanges, the reader will generally lack an in- depth knowledge of the writer's background which may be important to understanding her/his biases and silences. It may be useful for readers to know that while Rand argues that all decisions must be arrived at through a rational process that preserves the individual's life and happiness, she was dependent upon amphetamines and smoked two packs of cigarettes as day—which eventually led to her dying of lung cancer. The deep and often unconscious forces within the ecology of the physical, psychological, emotional energies, and impulses that circulate within the individual, as we often observe, make the life of self-centered rationality far more difficult and less pure than Rand acknowledges in her writings.

A crucial point lost on modern thinkers, including Rand, who relate human progress to a further expansion of capital markets is that the new digital technologies contribute to a massive loss of information. With the globalization of the printed word, this process of colonizing other cultures to adopt the idea that equates abstract knowledge with high-status knowledge is a particularly serious problem—one that is having its greatest impact on the youth who are increasingly dependent upon digitized communication. This is the point made by Wes Jackson in *Alters of Unhewn Stone: Science and the Earth* (1987). The information exchanged at the local level, from genes responding to the information circulating in the hierarchy of ecologies they are dependent upon, to the intergenerational knowledge and skills that sustain daily life in the cultural commons, to the information exchanges that occur as oceans become warmer and the melting of glaciers accelerates, are all examples of the connections between local contexts and the information to which the other participants in the cultural and natural ecologies respond.

As Jackson points out, the continual quest for new discoveries, ways of thinking, and technologies (including the accelerated speed at which abstract information can be spread) has led to ignoring the information vital to the self-renewing capacity of natural systems— including the intergenerational renewing of cultural traditions that have improved the quality, safety, patterns of mutual support, and social justice achievements that are too often taken for granted in society. (13-14) The massiveness of this loss of information can be assessed by considering how the growing dependence of youth and adults upon communicating through the digital technologies are major contributors to cultural amnesia, which involves the loss of awareness of the traditions we will most need in the future as we become even more dependent upon automation and existence in a surveillance society. Cultural amnesia, which most modern educators view as necessary for the emancipation of the individual, and which Rand and her fellow-travelers promote as contributing to a world of pure capitalism, is now viewed in a positive light. That is, it is thought to contribute to more freedom of the individual. What is not recognized is that given the rapid changes occurring in this century—with ecosystems being rapidly degraded, with the greater concentration of wealth and political power, with computer-driven automation making workers increasingly redundant, and with what remains of the cultural commons being rapidly integrated into the market systems—the cultural amnesia of the individual ensures that her/his civil liberties will become increasingly vulnerable to the forces of the corporate state.

The questions that people should be asking are about the losses and gains associated with the uses of various technologies, especially the new digital technologies that allow for the faster transfer of information abstracted from local cultural and environmental ecologies. While something as complex and pervasive as the connections between different technologies and the different ways in which they contribute to abstract and thus surface knowledge of local contexts, it would be wrong to place the blame on a single institution. Yet it is difficult to ignore the fact that public schools and universities, which represent sites where questions can be asked and historical forces examined, have failed in a number of ways. These include the failure to engage students in an examination of the cultural mediating characteristics of different technologies—including the mediating effects (gains and losses) of technologies that promote greater reliance upon print. Few students learn that technologies are not culturally neutral, and even fewer learn about the differences in how orality and literacy alter consciousness and social relationships. Nor are students encouraged to consider how print-based cultural storage and thinking foster a subjective form of individualism, as well as the cultural proclivity to ignore that everything ranging across all aspects of the cultural and natural ecologies in which we live out our lives involve relationships. The supposed autonomous individual, as pointed out earlier, is always a participant in an ecology of relationship—as plants animals, corporations, technologies, the built culture, languaging processes, and so forth—do not exist in a state of isolation. Everything is connected, and the nature of the behaviors of the participants in these ecologies need to be understood in terms of whether they are life enhancing or destroying.

Ayn Rand's world is a fiction that can only be taken as an accurate representation of the prospects of a life based on the rational pursuit of self-interest if readers do not understand that no degree of rational thinking can enable people to escape their responsibility for how their values and behaviors affect the well-being of others—including the environment. This understanding, which involves being aware of one's local contexts and patterns of interactions with others, will only come to those who begin to think in terms of the interdependencies between cultural and natural ecologies. The current emphasis on computer-mediated learning, where even the visual representations present only a surface and time-restricted understanding of contexts, and the spoken words (lectures) that have been largely influenced by what the professor has read, simply makes more difficult the transition to a greater reliance upon ecological intelligence—which is the exact opposite of what Rand has presented to her millions of readers. Ecological intelligence, as Bateson reminds us, involves basing our responses on a careful observation of the "differences which make a difference" as we interact with the Other, which may take the form of a conversation that is transformed into a dialogue, playing with a group of musicians or a game of chess, being aware of how behaviors affect natural systems and how the changes in natural systems affects the health of others, and so forth. It involves being aware of the multiple forms of information communicated through the relationships that are not recognized when intelligence is guided by abstract ideas and a view of the rational process that is not based on an understanding the shaping influence of the cultural ecology of language—which is one of the most primal and inescapable relationships.

References

Bateson, G. 1972. *Steps to an Ecology of Mind*. New York: Ballantine Books.
Goody, J. 2000. *The Power of the Written Tradition*. Washington, D. C.: Smithsonian Institution Press.
Havelock, E. 1986. *The Muse Learns to Write: Reflections on Orality and Literacy from Antiquity to the Present*. New Haven, Conn.: Yale University Press.
Lowenstein, R. 2012, "Is Any CEO Worth $189,000 Per Hours?" *Bloomberg Businessweek*. February 20-26. Pp. 8-9.
Jackson, W. 1987. *Alters of Unhewn Sone: Science and the Earth*. San Francisc, CA.: North Point Press.
Ong, W. 1982. *Orality and Literacy: The Technologizing of the Word*. New York. Methuen.
Rand, Ayn. 1961. *The Virtue of Selfishness*. New York; Signet.

Chapter 6

How the Coming Online Revolution in Higher Education Will Lead to the Elimination of Faculty

The world of higher education seems poised to enter a period of radical change: the onset of mass online education. Awash with excitement over this development, too many pundits are failing to discuss the cultural and ecological problems that the Internet revolution exacerbates. In a syndicated *New York Times* op-ed titled "Come the Revolution," Thomas Friedman extols this shift toward online education, citing the huge debt students are now taking on, especially when they study at elite universities such as Harvard or Stanford, and even at state universities. The convenience of taking online courses, especially when the cost is reduced to a hundred dollars per course, also gives credibility to Friedman's announcement of the coming revolution (actually, online university degrees have been offered for several decades, with the British Open University being a prime example).

Friedman cites the example of the new online platform developed by two professors at Stanford University, and how one of the originators, Andrew Ng, taught a course on machine learning that was taken by 100,000 students around the world. The low cost to students, the international reach of online courses, the prospects of obtaining a university degree without being burdened for life with a huge debt, the ability for students to interact with other students and with professors, the way in which student performance can be machine evaluated, how the low cost of online courses combined with tens of thousands of students hugely improves the finances of universities, and the elite nature of the universities now leading the revolution in making higher education available to more students all add to the impression of the Internet as contributing to yet another form of progress. But Friedman, like many others, fails to examine the cultural and ecological problems that the Internet revolution intensifies.

The Replacement of Workers by Machines

The combination of economic globalization and the increasing use of computer-driven machines have created a situation in which one professor can be responsible for an online course with an enrollment of tens of thousands of students. This global shift is akin to the earliest era of the Industrial Revolution, when power-driven machines reduced the number of workers using preindustrial technologies for carrying out a particular task. With the introduction of steam engines and power looms, the productivity of two or three low-paid workers became equal to what previously required the labor of several hundred workers. Indeed, the human desire to replace drudgery and mind-numbing repetitive behaviors has been one of the driving forces in the West that led to equating new technologies with the idea of progress. The profit motive has also been part of this effort to replace workers with machines. The coming Internet era of online degrees will continue this tradition of displacing workers, in this case professors and classroom teachers, with computer simulations and other online curricula.

A question now being asked in other sectors of society is, "Will a computer program drive the machine that takes away my job?" This question will lead students thinking about an academic career to consider whether the industrialization of learning will be intellectually challenging, and whether there is the prospect of lifetime employment. With the globalization of knowledge, which means online degree programs can be produced anywhere in the world and by institutions of widely varying standards, having a lifetime career becomes increasingly uncertain. This industrialization of learning will also influence both the time devoted to scholarly research and whether the product of that research can be packaged as on online course.

The more immediate question relates to whether online degrees will lead fewer students to enroll in the bricks-and-mortar campuses. A downturn in enrollment will, in turn, lead to laying off of faculty in programs that are seen as increasingly unsustainable economically and thus as archaic in the postmodern digital world. Faculty who lack the knowledge and skills to work in one of the trades, which are themselves undergoing changes due to the introduction of labor-saving and cost-cutting machines, may also fail to understand that participating in the local cultural commons represents the difference between life-threatening poverty and less money-dependent and toxic lifestyles. Today's cultural commons have many of the characteristics of the communities of the Luddites in early nineteenth-century England, which were destroyed by the first Industrial Revolution, that has now entered its digital phase of globalization. Unfortunately, the diversity of the world's cultural commons is being undermined by the digital revolution that Friedman views as so promising.

Print-Based Knowledge and Communication Contribute to Linguistic Colonization

Walter Ong, Jack Goody, and Eric Havelock have written extensively about the ways that print, given different cultural variables, leads to a form of consciousness different from that experienced in oral cultures. One of the key differences is that print-based knowledge, in not being able to accurately represent the flow of events and tacit understanding of local contexts, leads to a superficial knowledge of events, ideas, and experiences. Reliance on the senses, memory, and culturally acquired tacit understandings is more likely to be context-dependent. That is, for all its other advantages, print fosters abstract thinking that cannot take account of the depth of the culturally mediated experiences that exist in local contexts. For example, online courses require learning a way of thinking about events, procedures, and issues, and then imposing these abstract understandings (usually a theory that explains relationships and procedures) on the students' local cultural contexts. As online courses rely heavily on print as well as other abstract media, the widely held assumption that words have a universal meaning and that they name individual entities and events will be further reinforced.

Reliance on the printed word also reinforces the sender/receiver view of language (the conduit view of language that Michael Reddy writes about) that marginalizes awareness that most words are metaphors that carry forward the silences and misconceptions of earlier thinkers whose analogs continue to frame the meaning of words that are still taken for granted today.

For example, the reference to "machine learning," which is the title of the Stanford University online course taken by a hundred thousand students from different regions of the world, involves a radically different understanding of what constitutes "learning" than when this metaphor is used in other cultures. The privileging of print-based knowledge and communication over oral traditions also leads to abstract thinking in which there is no accountability between the use of the West's context-free metaphors—such as "freedom," "democracy," "free markets," "progress," and "individualism"––and the ecology of languages of other cultures. The West's context-free metaphors, which are so easily presented in print, have been used to justify both military and commercial forms of cultural imperialism.

What the computer scientists and technologists who write the computer programs are not likely to have encountered in their own education is that words are metaphors, and that the printed word gives few clues to how it's supposed current meanings were framed in the past by people who settled on analogs that are still carried forward and have become part of the computer scientists' taken-for-granted interpretative frameworks. This process of socialization should be understood as the linguistic colonization of the present by the past, which is largely ignored because of the many ways people have been indoctrinated with the belief that they are autonomous thinkers. These misconceptions are further reinforced when what is learned in an online course is encoded in print, in videos that are also abstractions from the world of living cultural and natural ecologies, and by the cultural amplifications and reductions that are inherent characteristics of computers. And when the mode of abstract representation (i.e., print, visual, auditory) becomes the basis of thinking for students from non-Western cultures, the online course, taught in whichever Western language, becomes a form of cultural colonization. As most computer programmers ignore this characteristic of the printed word, there are few instances in which the content of the online course challenges students to consider the cultural differences in the meaning of words. Instead of reflecting on the cultural ecology of the vocabulary and other abstract visual images appearing on the screen, the student is more likely to consider them as factual and objective representations of how to think about reality––especially when the online course is part of a degree program offered by universities such as Stanford, MIT, and other elite institutions.

How Abstract Systems of Representation Undermine Our Ecological Intelligence

As Ong and other linguists focusing on the differences between orality and literacy have pointed out, the idea that print-based knowledge and communication are more accurate and objective also reinforces the privileging of sight over the other senses--which in turn strengthens the idea of being an autonomous individual who sees, thinks, and acts. Indeed, one of the arguments used to promote the wider use of computers in education is that they provide access to data, information, and accounts that far exceeds what the classroom teacher or professor can bring to the student's learning experience. The further claim for computer-mediated learning is that it adds to the ability of students to construct their own knowledge--which is an argument that fails to consider that students' thought processes are largely dependent on the metaphorical vocabulary they acquire when becoming a member of a language community. During the early stages of language acquisition, the child is vulnerable to accepting word meanings (metaphors) that carry forward the misconceptions, insights, and silences of the people whose analogs continue to frame those meanings. As this process of learning is largely taken for granted, few attend to the way that the history of words reproduces earlier ways of thinking that do not take into account the current cultural and natural ecologies that vary in terms of ethnic groups, bioregions, and metanarratives. To summarize the key misconception reinforced by the privileging of the abstract knowledge encoded in print, it is that there is such an entity as an autonomous thinker and actor. This culturally specific assumption and the assumption about the objective nature of knowledge communicated through print are likely to be reinforced across the courses made available as part of an online degree.

The reality, as Gregory Bateson points out, is that everything exists in relationships with other participants in cultural and natural ecologies. That is, individuals, plants, animals, genes, macroclimate systems, and so forth always exist in complex and interdependent communications systems we call ecologies. The printed word is unable to represent the dynamic, interactive, and ongoing communication of information that Bateson suggests can be understood as the "difference which makes a difference" circulating through all ecologies. What

Bateson is arguing is that "differences," especially when we are aware of them, lead to differences in our response, which in turn lead to differences to which other participants, ranging from genes to macroecosystems, in the cultural and natural ecology respond to--in an ongoing process. The assumption that things exist in some kind of an autonomous status or as fixed entities—represented in the assumption that there are independent facts, objective data, and events that can be understood as separate from the differences which make a difference circulating through interactive ecologies—is also reinforced through print-encoded knowledge. What students are not likely to learn in these online courses is how to recognize how the language that is the basis of their taken-for-granted patterns of thinking fails to accurately represent the cultural and natural ecological systems in which they are embedded. And it is unlikely that any of the online courses, even those created by scholars with international reputations, will challenge students to identify new culturally and ecologically informed analogs that will overcome the problem of how words (metaphors) continue to reproduce earlier culturally specific misconceptions and silences. For example, how many students from other cultures who are in the early stages of learning English are going to be aware that the current meanings of such pervasively used metaphors as "freedom," "individualism," "progress," "data," " technology," "development," were framed in earlier eras when there was no awareness of environmental limits? The ethnocentrism of these earlier eras is also reproduced in the current use of these metaphors.

Playing tennis, preparing a soufflé, writing a paragraph, talking with a stranger or friend, planting a garden, deciding how to dress given a change in the weather, going to war, performing in an orchestra, promoting social reforms, and introducing a new technology such as literacy or computers all involve varying degrees of awareness of differences— that is, the information already being exchanged within the local and macronatural and cultural ecologies. The conceptual maps acquired from print-based learning, that is, abstract learning reinforced in these online courses, undermine the ability to give full attention to the differences (information circulating, as Foucault would put it, as an 'action upon an action' of the Other)—which in turn introduces differences that make a difference within the interactive fields of relationships. This results in the introduction of policies, procedures, and technologies that are often poorly suited to the local characteristics of different natural and cultural ecologies. A good example of the failure of abstract thinking on the part of highly literate and thus abstract-thinking politicians is the way the borders of countries were established during the colonial era. Their decisions failed to take into account local contexts (cultural and natural ecologies)—that is, the tribal and religious groups holding opposing ideas that have now become the basis of today's political conflicts. This can also be seen in the development of infrastructure systems that have failed to take into account the cultural practices of local communities—freeways and the location of centers of political power would be prime examples.

Computer-driven technologies that displace the need for workers, who are needed by the economic system to consume what can now be more efficiently produced, provide yet another example of how abstract thinking, rather than ecological thinking, leads to double binds that have dire social consequences.

What is not likely to be understood by the people who turn the knowledge of various disciplines into online courses is that the vocabulary (again, context-free printed words) used in a course influences which differences that make a difference will become the focus of the student's attention and will thus be taken into account in the student's response. To make this point more directly, a vocabulary that reinforces the misconception of being an autonomous, rationally directed individual will lead to a person-centered form of ecological intelligence in which the only differences that make a difference to be taken into account will be those related to the individual's personal agenda.

For example, the person trying to find the opening on the flow of traffic that will allow getting ahead of other drivers gives attention and responds to a limited set of differences: the space between the cars in the lane the person wants to move into, the speed of the slower vehicle just ahead, the weather conditions, and so forth. This person-centered exercise of ecological intelligence does not take account of potential destructive impact on others or on the natural systems that result from driving a car with a high carbon footprint. An online course, in reinforcing the Western assumption that what is learned adds to the individual's capacity to be an autonomous rational thinker, further contributes to a society that is unable to recognize that the Western view of the autonomous individual is partly at the root of the ecological crisis. When few professors outside the sciences take the ecological crisis seriously enough to examine how their own courses reinforce the same deep cultural assumptions that contribute to overshooting the sustaining capacity of natural systems, their behavior further ensures that online courses will be able to address only technological solutions caused by cultural assumptions that are little understood. Unfortunately, the education of most scientists is also limiting in that it failed to address how print reinforces abstract thinking and thus limits the exercise of ecological intelligence. Perhaps more important, the education of most scientists fails to introduce them to the understanding that metaphorical language reproduces the misconceptions of earlier eras, which can be seen in how their culturally dictated understanding of progress has precluded them from considering the importance of what their new technologies are displacing.

What Is Lost Through Computer-Mediated Learning

Friedman refers to the dawning of the era of Internet university degrees in metaphors that make questioning the "revolutionary" developments of Professor Ng and other proponents of online degrees appear reactionary. Isn't it sheer ignorance to question what Friedman refers to as the "top quality" and "world class" learning that will be made available by the professors from Stanford, Michigan, Princeton, and other elite universities?

What is too often overlooked because of the late twentieth-century education of most professors who will write these supposedly world-class online courses is the simple insight of the late Theodore Roszak, who noted that the basic relationship in computer-mediated learning is the mind of the student meeting the minds of the people who write the software. While the professor writing the online course may have an outstanding scholarly record, that professor will too often reproduce the silences and misconceptions shared within the discipline, as well as the taken-for-granted language and thus the culturally specific root metaphors that have guided the process of modernization and now globalization.

What continues to be overlooked is that the graduates of these elite universities have become the power brokers on Wall Street and the foreign policy experts who have sent the youth of the middle and poorer classes into one war after another. To date, the graduates of these elite universities continue to promote economic globalization and the further development of technologies that reduce the need for workers. Their understanding of what constitutes progress and wealth, which is driven largely by abstract ideologies inherited from the print-based thinking of earlier western thinkers, is in many instances the basis of social policies that are contributing to the spread of poverty and the further degradation of natural systems.

While Friedman celebrates the way that the elite universities will package and make available their high-status knowledge, the real problems that will dominate the lives of students from all regions of the world will be the deepening ecological crisis that is already threatening sources of protein and potable water, causing changes in habitats, and increasing disruptions in civil society as the forces of economic globalization further undermine the life-sustaining ability of natural systems. How many computer scientists such as Professor Ng, and how many of the social science and humanities faculty at these elite universities, are aware of how their thinking is based on many of the same deep, taken-for-granted cultural assumptions that provided conceptual and moral legitimacy for the industrial culture that is still being promoted as the engine of progress? Asking the same questions about the misconceptions, silences, and cultural colonization that are part of any regular face-to-face class that also involves textbooks, which will be magnified by a largely print-based online course of study, brings into focus the highly problematic nature of Friedman's claim of a world-class education, as well as that of his claim that the online revolution in higher education represents the best that the elite universities have to offer.

Who Will Receive the Monetary Benefits from Online Courses?

The economy of scale appears to benefit the students (who obtain credit for completing a low-cost online course), the universities that own the copyright, as well as the corporations that maintain the online delivery. In other words, huge profits are to be made. Given Professor Ng's example of offering a course taken by 100,000 students, and the claim that already over a million students have taken other online courses, it's clear that economic forces will soon lead university administrators to terminate unpopular programs and to reduce the number of campus-based faculty.

Will the profits from the new system be made available in the form of a safety net for those faculty who have been dismissed as redundant? Will the faculty member who creates the online course receive fair compensation, or will the salary paid during the time it took to create the online course be considered adequate? And what should be the response of faculty unions to the challenges posed by turning online university degrees into a new large and highly profitable industry? Their response will likely focus on economic issues, as few faculty possess the conceptual background necessary for challenging the threat posed by the inherent culturally mediating characteristics of computers to further undermine the development of ecological intelligence needed in the years ahead.

Another question that has yet to be answered is how many faculty members will be able to raise equally critical questions about the ways that online courses, especially those taught in English, undermine cultures that have survived in harsh environments by developing ecological intelligence and encoding it in their languages. Instead of engaging faculty in the computer sciences about the forms of knowledge and skill development that cannot be acquired from an online course, the dominant mood among faculty is more like the frog that fails to recognize the dangers of sitting in a pot that is heating up. When university administrators decide that online courses create more revenue than departments with declining enrollments and tenure can no longer protect the faculty from being laid off, it will be (as with the frog in the boiling water) too late.

Friedman holds out the promise that the delivery systems in this emerging era of online degrees will enable students in different regions of the world to encounter the best minds that the elite universities have to offer. But there is little evidence that these world-class faculty members understand the nature and ecological importance of the world's diversity of cultural commons and how they are being undermined by computer-mediated learning. Would they be able to engage computer science faculty in an extended discussion of the printed word's inherent ethnocentricity and its reproduction of the deep cultural assumptions that are partly at the root of the ecological crisis? Would they be able to clarify why the spoken word, communal memory, and reliance on all the senses as sources of information have enabled some cultures to develop ecologically sustainable daily practices? The even more difficult challenge would be to engage computer science faculty in a way that would facilitate their openness to learning what they do not know. The combination of specialized languages and the hubris that comes with promoting cutting-edge technologies makes interdisciplinary exchanges exceedingly difficult.

The one point that faculty in the social sciences and humanities would be able to make is that online courses, unlike courses with similar course titles that provide students with a wide range of interpretations, would promote the interpretation of the professor or expert who prescribes what the course content should be. Economic and technological factors will dictate that the course content be free of ambiguities and alternative interpretations that would limit the ability to machine-score the students' performance. This, in turn, raises the question of whether computer science faculty understand the dangers of courses that promote a monocultural mentality, and whether university administrators will be able to resist the economic benefits of offering the same online course over and over again.

Moral Double-Binds Produced by the Industrialization of Higher Education

As it becomes clearer to students that obtaining an online degree from a major university both provides the credential they need for competing for employment in an economy that needs fewer workers and also leaves them facing the uncertainties of employment with a smaller burden of debt, traditional universities will likely face rapidly declining enrollments. This, in turn, will confront faculty, especially in departments whose curricula do not relate directly to promoting economic and technological development, with a moral double bind. That is, in order to avoid the dismissal of faculty in departments that have declining enrollments, faculty members have traditionally encouraged students to pursue academic interests that align with the interests of the faculty. The encouragement has usually been accompanied by vague assurances that the graduate student's years of study will be rewarded with some form of employment in higher education. The vagueness of this promise will now disappear as the stark reality of widespread unemployment among faculty can no longer be denied.

As a result the faculty will face this moral issue: Do they continue to encourage students to pursue graduate study in their department (which will help to preserve their own jobs), or do they warn students that their years of study may not be rewarded with future employment in a field related to their specialized area of study? Some students may be willing to pursue their intellectual interests regardless of future economic consequences. But it is likely that more students will elect to adapt their intellectual interests to what will enable them to earn a living—which will lead to a decline in student enrollments followed by administrative decisions to reduce the number of faculty or to cancel programs entirely. In the background will be the reality that the institution's budget will be expanding as more students adopt the online route to a university degree.

A Slippery Political Slope

We are reminded daily that most computer scientists—like their colleagues in the sciences whose students reproduce the silences of their mentors by working for a chemical industry that produces billions of pounds of pesticides and other toxins each year—give little thought to the cultural and ecological consequences that ripple outward from their latest technological innovations. Their education is too specialized to engage in any in-depth examination of the moral and political implications of the technologies that are reducing the need for workers, and these technologies are bringing the lives of everyone under the surveillance networks that benefit corporations and the growing fascist tendencies of government to monitor people's activities in order to anticipate crimes and acts of disloyalty. These issues are not likely to be addressed by the "world class" professors who will be developing online curricula in the sciences and related technology fields.

There is another problem that also needs to be considered as more students sign up for online degrees in order to avoid a life of crushing indebtedness. As demonstrated by the Stanford University example of tens of thousands of students taking the same course, and as we are learning about the government's massive surveillance of people's everyday activities, taking an online course leads to more than a grade based on a machine-scored test. It also provides others, ranging from the government to potential employers and even other citizens, a record of the ideas students encounter in the online courses—as well as their performance. If an employer wants to hire a graduate of an online program from one of the elite universities and the data reveal that the content of one of the courses included exposure to Keynesian economics and a critique of capitalism, it is very likely that the student will not be hired--regardless of what the student has come to think about the merits of Keynesian economics and the merits of capitalism.

Similarly, if students were to protest in Luddite fashion the further industrialization of their educational experience, this too would become part of the data-based profile of the student's character and potential for politically disruptive behavior. Just as we are now awash in the thousands of toxic chemicals introduced into the environment by scientists in the name of progress, we are also awash in data that represent highly abstracted evidence of people's thoughts and actions--again, in the name of progress. Without the benefit of knowing the context out of which the data are derived and the individual's own explanations, people making decisions about employment, security risks, loans for housing, and other activities will impose their own ideological biases on what the data mean. The wrong kind of data, or an irresponsible interpretation of the data, now serve as an indictment, especially when ideological, ethnic, and religious issues become part of interpreting what the data means. Unlike the old system of being able to defend oneself, being able to question the evidence that is the basis of the indictment, and being judged by a jury of peers, the new online system will lead to politically and economically adverse decisions that will never reach the courtroom, where the old safeguards still survive. As the late eighteenth-century philosopher Jeremy Bentham understood, in a panopticon-designed prison where everyone is under constant surveillance, the prisoners will begin to self-police their own actions. This same phenomenon of self-policing will become more widespread as computer-mediated activities lead to the massive accumulation of data to be used by anonymous others in centers of power.

For all of these reasons, we need to be wary of pundits such as Friedman who obfuscate the complexity of changes in an ecologically stressed and multicultural world. By extolling of the industrialization of education with god-words such as "breakthroughs," "hyperconnected," "revolutionary," they position themselves on the side of the winners in the process of economic and technological globalization.

Chapter 7

Is Using Computers in Oral Cultures a Cultural Affirming Technology or a Trojan Horse?

Promoting literacy in oral cultures has been a long-time objective of different groups in the West, from religious missionaries, politicians who wanted to bring non-western cultures under the control of western-style governments, and corporations driven by the awareness that literacy is essential to selling their products. The most recent development in this long history of stamping out illiteracy, and the supposedly primitive consciousness that goes with it, is the current effort to promote the use of Internet technologies. This was the purpose of Nicholas Negroponte's efforts a decade ago to make inexpensive and rugged computers available to the world's children. Intel and other computer corporations have also made their technology available to children in different regions of the world with the expectation that this would promote literacy, a computer-dependent lifestyle, and brand loyalty.

It is important to understand how the phrase "oral cultures" is being used here, especially since all cultures rely upon the spoken words for maintaining relationships and sharing knowledge and expectations with others. In one sense all cultures could be classified as oral cultures, but the distinction I am making in the use of this phrase is to separate those that treat literacy as having higher status from cultures where the spoken word is the primary means of storing knowledge and for maintaining the affairs of daily life. This distinction is not meant as an absolute, but as a way of identifying differences in degrees of emphasis. Many cultures that fit the category of oral cultures may have their own systems of writing, but their reliance on print for communicating and record keeping falls far short of how print has become the dominant and now most reliable system for communicating, record keeping, and establishing the factual and objective status of what is being communicated. In terms of these general differences, the oral cultures are mostly in the so-called "undeveloped" regions of the world. Being identified as "undeveloped" is largely based on the West's tradition of associating literacy with being developed, and the lack of literacy with being "undeveloped."

When I refer to oral cultures I am mindful of this long-standing pattern of thinking, and that most oral cultures would also be identified as being part of the Third World. I am also mindful that in the so-called developed cultures there are cultures that have retained their oral traditions even in the face of efforts to transform them into the abstract, individualist thinkers that accompanies reliance upon the printed word. In the following discussion of the continuing efforts to promote literacy and to bringing these preliterate cultures into the modern world of digital communication, I include the indigenous cultures of North and South America, New Zealand and Australia, regions of South East Asia, India, Africa, and the northern regions of Europe and Russia. The primary focus on this latest effort to promote the West's approach to literacy is on how digital technologies (which requires the ability to read) are being promoted especially among the youth of these cultures. It is well understood that this is the group most susceptible to abandoning the old ways, and to becoming addicted to a consumer-dependent lifestyle even when the jobs necessary to support this lifestyle are not available.

The most recent effort to bring the supposedly backward youth in oral cultures into the modern consumer-dependent world is the Worldreader project that has its home-base in San Francisco, California. This time, the technology being distributed mostly in Africa is the digital reader, with thousands of Kindles being handed out to children who will undergo a transformation to a print-based western consciousness. As Nicholas Carr points out in his book, *The Shallows: What the Internet is Doing to Our Brains* (2011), digital technologies undermine long-term memory, foster an addiction to finding the latest exciting image or bit of news, and substituting the subjective choices of the individual for the communal memory of the injustices done to others and the genuine achievements of the past. In short, it undermines awareness of environmental and cultural interdependencies, while making the oral traditions that carry forward the moral values and identity of the culture obstacles that can be made to disappear from consciousness with a click on the keyboard. Not mentioned by Carr is that digital storage and communication rely upon print and other abstract systems of representations—even while they create the impression of capturing reality in ways that surpass the printed word.

This long history of promoting literacy, and now digital-based literacy, among cultures that have relied on face-to-face communication as the primary way of intergenerational renewal of the cultural commons, has been driven by the idea that literacy and now the ability to participate in cyberspace is essential to promoting individualism and the other cultural assumptions that lead to a consumer-dependent lifestyle. Whether the western form of consciousness is ecologically sustainable, and whether it enables members of the community to carry forward the intergenerational knowledge and skills that sustains the cultural and environmental commons is not being considered. Indeed, in the earliest eras of literacy-based cultural colonization, as well as in the current digital phase of colonization, the dominant idea was that there are no limits on social and technological progress. That technologies are not culturally neutral, and that they often degrade both the environment and human possibilities, was also not considered.

There are fundamental differences between the digital impact on Native American youth, the youth in a Peruvian village, and the youth in villages across Africa where e-books are now being distributed. Yet the similarities are profoundly important. The most important one is that they are all experiencing the loss of intergenerational knowledge as computers are introduced into their classrooms, and as they rely more on abstract (that is, digital) systems of communication. And they are all experiencing the ways in which print-based storage, now magnified by the speed of digital technologies that overcome the previous barriers of space and time, are contributing to the cultural amnesia that is becoming a characteristic of the western/modern style individual. The following examination of the arguments for and against the use of computers in the classrooms of Native Americans highlights the issues that should be the focus of discussions in other cultures where the digital revolution is now beginning to undermine the oral traditions of non-western cultures.

There is a long and well-documented history of how schooling, with its emphasis on print-based knowledge, was used to transform the oral-based consciousness of the indigenous cultures spread across North America. But it has only been in the last 30 or so years that the role of computers in this process of cultural colonization has become part of the ongoing debate within these cultures. In many instances, the speed with which the youth of these culture have embraced each new digital technology has made these debates, especially those appearing in print, less useful in deciding which technologies to accept and which to reject. Nevertheless, it is important to consider these debates as they raise questions that should be considered in other cultures. As the combination economic/technological globalization and the rapid degradation in the viability of natural systems threaten the sources of food, water, and group solidarity, the impact of the abstract and individualistic thinking promoted by digital technologies on the renewal of the cultural and environmental commons will become increasingly important.

While the debate had been going on for some time, an article by Craig Howe that appeared in the *Wicazo Sa Review* clearly framed the issues as well as the decision Howe thought should be made about using computers in reservation classrooms. "The Internet" he warned "is an exceedingly deceptive technology whose power is immensely attractive to American Indians. But until its universalistic and individualistic foundation is restructured to incorporate spatial, social, spiritual, and experiential dimensions that particularize its application, cyberspace is no place for tribalism" (1988, p. 27). This warning, however, continues to go unheeded by educators, linguists, and some tribal leaders who see in the computer a means of regenerating the language and traditional knowledge essential to tribal identity. As elders pass on, the tribal knowledge encoded in a CD-ROM appears safe from going extinct. The Tewa Language Project CD-ROM, the classroom use of computers adapted to the characteristics of the Hawaiian language, and the use of computers in Native classrooms for purposes of exchanging ideas within the "global village" represent just a few of the efforts that ignored Howe's warning about the Janus nature of computers.

While Howe observed that computers are the latest "foreign good" that encode the western ideal of individualism (p. 26) and a rootless form of existence, most educators continue to justify the use of computers in Native classrooms on grounds that echo the arguments being used in the dominant culture. David Lewis, for example, explained the educational gains for the Naskapi students (who live 1000 miles north of Quebec City) in the following way:

> The rationale for using technology involving traditions and culture, and therefore the community, is to interest and motivate the students, bring the school and community closer together, create needed resources for the community, and enhance understanding between students, staff, and other people in the community. p. 31

He concluded a brief discussion of how some members of the community view modern technology as undermining traditional ways with the statement that "it all depends on how the technology is used." In other words, the technology, including computers, are culturally neutral.

Similarly, in writing about how the networked classroom helped Hawaiian students learn their native language and other cultural traditions, Constance Hale made the claim that computers represent "a medium perhaps better suited to an oral tradition than the book ever was" (1995, p. 4). And in a conversation I had with two university graduates who were working with the village elders in the Sierra de Juarez mountains of Oaxaca in helping the youth learn to solve current problems on the basis of ancestral knowledge, I was told that the computer is a culturally neutral technology. As one of the graduate students put it, "the purpose of the user determines whether it is a constructive or destructive force."

As the above statements suggest, the advocates of using computers in Native classrooms needed to reflect more deeply on the culture transforming effects of this technology and, in the process, engage the fundamental issues that Howe raises—issues that need to be framed in terms of the cultural forms of knowledge and community that have a smaller ecological footprint than that of the technologically dependent dominant culture. In order to facilitate this deeper level of reflection and discussion among educators, as well as within the councils of elders, and among members of the community, the issues raised in a scholarly body of literature (Ihde, 1979; Winograd and Flores, 1986; Roszak, 1994; Carr, 2011, Bowers, 1993, 1995, 1997, 2000, 2011), will need to become the focus for these discussions.. It is also hoped that the analysis of these issues will bring into question the wisdom of training teachers in the various applications of computers but not in helping them understand how computers contribute to undermining the cultural diversity that represents an alternative to a global consumer and technologically dependent monoculture. Lastly, as this analysis should be viewed as clarifying relationships and issues that have not been part of the literature on educational computing, it is hoped that others will extend those parts of the analysis that have only been briefly touched upon, and extend the analysis in directions that have been overlooked.

In order to avoid being prejudged as anti-computer, it must be acknowledge at the outset the many ways computers have been highly useful in maintaining the networks of communication among indigenous groups, and thus helping to increase their effectiveness in the political arena. The ability of the indigenous people of Chiapas to focus worldwide attention on their political demands, as well as on the efforts of the Mexican government to suppress them, is perhaps one of the more prominent examples of the political effectiveness of computers, which is now being bypassed by other social media technologies.

As computers and other digital technologies become integrated into more aspects of economic life, competency in their use does indeed become essential to finding employment. The claim that computers will help Native students as well as students in non-western cultures learn about their cultural traditions is, as suggested earlier, more questionable. While the computer industry has multi-billion dollar reasons for maintaining the myth that computers are a culturally neutral technology, educators, politicians, and large segments of the general public not only continue to perpetuate this misconception but fail to recognize how the myth hides the transformation of consciousness that equates the continual spread of the Industrial Revolution with progress. It is this linkage that will be examined here. It is also important to clarify how the integration of computer-mediated learning with the changing needs of the workplace also leads to the loss of important forms of knowledge and communal relationships that are Howe's central concerns.

As one of the main arguments here is that computer-mediated learning reinforces the same cultural transforming patterns that were essential to the Industrial Revolution, it is necessary to digress momentarily from the main line of discussion in order to highlight one of the most fundamental cultural changes necessary for the creation of a consumer, individually-centered form of culture. In *Rebels Against the Future: The Luddites and Their War Against the Industrial Revolution* (1995), Kirkpatrick Sale notes that all that "community" implies—self-sufficiency, mutual aid, morality in the marketplace, stubborn tradition, regulation by custom, organic knowledge instead of mechanistic science—had to be steadily and systematically disrupted and displaced. *All of the practices that kept the individual from being a consumer* had to be done away with so that the cogs and wheels of an unfettered machine called 'the economy' could operate without interference, influenced merely by invisible hands and inevitable balances.... p. 38. (italics added)

In short, the industrial model required not only the elimination of the traditional market that was generally limited to a specific day of the week and to being held in a particular locality within the community, it also required an autonomous individual who, in lacking personal skills and interdependent relationships within the community, would be dependent upon manufactured goods and expert services. This transformation continues to be encoded in the modern way of equating greater individual autonomy, consumerism, and technological development with progress. It is also expressed in such recent technological developments as e-commerce which connects the manufacturer directly to consumers by excluding the need for small community centered enterprises.

Today, the myth of technology as a culturally neutral tool hides the fact that we are entering the digital phase of the Industrial Revolution that is speeding up the process of globalizing consumerism and the increasing dependency on technology. Both of these trends undermine local knowledge. This connection between computers and the other technologies that make the Internet such a culturally transforming force create a special challenge for cultures attempting to maintain their traditions of community and spiritual connectedness. As pointed out earlier, computers contribute to economic and political gains, but at the same time they are a cultural transforming technology. What they reinforce is the modern, western pattern of individually-centered relations and the form of consciousness Sale described as essential to the earlier phase of the Industrial Revolution. How life in the Internet culture now contributes to the loss of historical memory, which Nicholas Carr describes in his recent book *The Shallow*, also undermines what is most essential to democratic decision making: namely, the ability to recognized what needs to be conserved as well as changed.

The increasing dependency upon computers in nearly every aspect of daily life, from communication, transportation, to health care, makes it difficult to argue that students should be isolated from a knowledge of how to use computers. But this growing dependency, along with the regeneration of the awareness among cultures of the importance of traditional knowledge of communal relationships, makes it all the more essential to understand the culturally transforming nature of computers. This understanding, in turn, makes it possible to recognize more clearly the appropriate and inappropriate uses of computers, as well as how computers enable certain groups to gain power and economic advantage over others.

Just as the printed word has a long history of being represented as a culturally neutral technology, while also being understood as overcoming the backwardness of pre-literate cultures, computers are also being represented as possessing these dual qualities. A careful examination of the forms of personal experience and cultural patterns they reinforce reveals something entirely different. Expanding upon Martin Heidegger's (1977) observations about the mediating characteristics of technology, Don Ihde notes that humans have three fundamental ways of experiencing technology: as background in a field of relationships (technologies that control temperature, sounds, light in a room, etc.), as interacting with a technology (switches, gear levers, key boards, etc.), and as a mediated experience where the nature of the technology amplifies certain aspects of individual/cultural experience while reducing or eliminating others (1979, pp. 53-65). For example, the way in which the characteristics of a technology select certain aspects of experience for amplification and reduction can be seen in how the nature of the stick amplifies a person's ability to reach into the higher branches while marginalizing the other aspects of embodied experience such as smell, taste, sound, and so forth. A second example can be seen in how the nature of the cell phone projects voice over vast distances while eliminating the non-verbal messages so important in interpersonal communication. Similarly, it is the nature of the computer that determines the patterns of thinking, communicating, and experiencing that will be reinforced as well as the patterns that will be marginalized or represented as non-existent.

One of the characteristics of the computer that contributes to its existential/cultural amplification characteristics is that it carries forward the cultural patterns associated with print—which many scholars have associated with a modern form of consciousness. (Goody, 1977; Ong, 1977, 1982; Havelock, 1986; Tannen, 1986) As these scholars have observed, given certain cultural variables, print represents reality as being separate from the reader, and thus reinforces the form of consciousness associated with the autonomous form of individualism where personal perspective, analysis, and decisions are considered the most valid sources of knowledge. The spoken word cannot be recovered with the same accuracy as the printed word, and thus does not lend itself to critical analysis which, along with the act of reading, is an individualized activity. In effect, the printed word (which can only provide a superficial account of the interactive and tacit nature of cultural contexts) has been represented by western thinkers as a more accurate representation of reality than the spoken word—which is dependent upon a knowledge of local contexts and interpersonal accountability. (Goody, 1977) Indeed, the privileging of print over the living reality of the spoken word has been an important source of past oppression in Native and Euro-American relationships. Computer mediated thinking and communication further exaggerates the cultural patterns inherent in print technology. It does this partly by the way in which advocates of computers treat oral and print-based communication as identical, and by their emphasis on identifying computer mediated communication and thought with participating in global networks—as though all the participants share an identical cultural epistemology.

The argument being presented here, that computers reinforce the rootless form of individualism described by Sale, needs further clarification as some readers may interpret it in a way that is not meant here. That is, it is <u>not</u> being claimed here that the form of individualism reinforced by computers prevents people from connecting with others in electronic communities. Indeed, this occurs—and computer mediated communication may even enable some individuals to share personal concerns with others in the electronic community that they cannot share on a personal, face-to-face basis. The more important point about how computers reinforce a modern form of individualism is stated in the most effective way by the early leading advocates of computers. For example, Sherry Turkle, the author of *The Second Self: Computers and the Human Spirit* (1987), and *Life on the Screen: Identify in the Age of the Internet* (1995), explained the connection between computers and individualism in the following way:

> I have argued that Internet experiences help us to develop models of
> psychological well-being that are in a meaningful sense postmodern:
> They admit of multiplicity and flexibility. They acknowledge the
> constructed nature of reality, self, and other. The Internet is not alone
> in encouraging such models. There are many places within our culture
> that do so. What they have in common is that they all suggest the
> value of approaching one's story in several ways and with fluid access to
> one's different aspec*ts. We are encouraged to think of ourselves as fluid,
> emergent, decentralized, multiplicitous, flexible, and ever in process.* pp.
> 263-264 (italics added)

While the computer allows people to share thoughts, information,
and engage in problem solving with others, the form of individual
subjectivity that it amplifies is profoundly different from the forms
of moral reciprocity found in face-to-face, and intergenerationally
centered communities. Harold Rheingold, one of the original members
of the electronic community in the San Francisco area called the
WELL, gives an account of his own personal experience that highlights
this difference:

> On top of the technology-imposed constraints, we who populate
> cyberspace deliberately experiment with fracturing traditional notions
> of identity by living in multiple simultaneous personae in different
> virtual neighborhoods. We reduce and encode our identities in words
> on a screen, decode and unpack the identities of others. The way we
> use these words, in stories (true and false) we tell about ourselves
> (or about the identities we want people to believe us to be) is what
> determines our identities in cyberspace. 1993, p. 61

In her most recent book, *AloneTogether: Why We expect More From
Technology and Less From Ourselves* (2011) Turkle reverses her earlier
views by claiming that the Internet promotes superficial relationships
and commitments disconnected from the values of the community.

The supposedly autonomous and experimental nature of
individualism fostered by print-based communication, which is
facilitated by the amplification characteristics of computers and
other digital technologies (including the speed of interaction that
simulates only the time element in the interactive nature of face-to-face
communication) is profoundly different from the forms of individualism
found in many oral cultures. An example of this difference is brought out
in Keith Basso's description of the form of subjectivity that accepts the
guidance of ancestors, and the moral lessons encoded in place names.

In *Wisdom Sits in Places: Language and Landscape Among the Western Apaches* (1996), Basso notes that for the Apaches from Cibecue

> the past lies embedded in the features of the earth—in canyons and lakes, mountains and arroyos, rocks and vacant fields—which together endow their lands with multiple forms of significance that reach into their lives and shape the way they think. Knowledge of places is therefore closely linked to knowledge of self, to grasping one's position in the larger scheme of things, including one's own community, and to securing a confident sense of who one is as a person. p. 34

The stories connected with place names, and which morally connect the present generation with the experiences (the 'path' or 'trail') of the ancestors, are part of an oral rather than a print tradition of communication. The form of individualism celebrated in Turkle's earlier books and by Rhiengold cannot experience these ancestral reference points in cyberspace. Again, the argument here is that the culture transforming nature of computers and other digital technologies has to do with the forms of intergenerational communication and embodied experiences that these technologies cannot reproduce—except in a de-contextualized way that fundamentally changes a form of community participation and renewal into the act of reading a text as an objective and detached individual. The vast resources available on the Internet do not necessarily lead to broadly informed ways of thinking as the individual exercises control over what she/he will access. This easily leads to the condition of cultural amnesia that is becoming a more prominent feature of modern life.

One of the double binds associated with how computers continue the tradition of representing print as a more progressive form of cultural storage than the oral tradition is that the rapid rate of technological innovation has diverted most people from asking about the forms of knowledge and communal relationships that are being undermined by this technology. The ecological significance of this double bind becomes even clearer when the ecological foot print of the autonomous and thus consumer dependent individual is compared with the ecological foot print of the individual who participates in the non-consumer oriented, intergenerational activities of a community that possesses the characteristics that Sale viewed as being undermined by the Industrial Revolution.

In spite of the many beneficial uses of computers and other digital technologies, the questions that must be asked by groups struggling to preserve communal traditions in the face of the relentless pressure to become a modern society of consumer-oriented individuals should include the following: What cultural patterns are being reinforced when, for instance, Choctaw students attending Red Water School in Carthage, Mississippi participate in on-line conversations with Navajo students attending Cottonwood Day School, and with students attending other reservation schools across North America? What changes in cultural ways of thinking, values, and interaction are reinforced when students are engaged in computer-based learning or texting students in other cultures? Do these forms of communication weaken the culturally specific patterns that form networks of mutual support so essential to communities that have not been totally turned into niche markets by corporations?

When students use the computer, their pattern of thinking must adapt to the requirements of the machine, and to the thought patterns of the people who write the software. A critical relationship overlooked by those who view computers as a neutral technology was made explicit by Theodore Roszak when he wrote in *The Cult of Information* (1994 edition) that the basic relationship between the student and the computer screen is "mind meeting mind." He goes on to point out that the "subliminal lesson that is being taught whenever the computer is used (unless a careful effort is made to offset that effect) is the data processing model of the mind." (p. 241) This model of thinking, which is now being further reinforced by the learning theorists who argue that students should construct their own understanding of relationships, corresponds to the conceptual patterns taken-for-granted in the dominant western culture. Furthermore, this model of thinking tends not to recognize what is specific to a particular cultural group. Thus, the shaping influence of computers goes largely unnoticed, particularly when the user assumes that the computer is a culturally neutral technology. In connecting this discussion more directly to the use of computers in reservation classrooms it is important to recognize that when students attending Red River School use a computer, regardless of whether it's a chat room, a simulated decision-making program such as SimCity, or the retrieving of information from a data base, they will experience themselves and the surrounding world in the following way—which are dictated by the cultural amplification and reduction characteristics of the computer.

(1) Decisions about which aspects of cyberspace they will become involved with will be experienced as an autonomous choice. That is, the computer involves an isolated experience of interacting with abstractions (words, pictures, graphs, etc.) that appear on the screen. Unlike face-to-face communication, the student is alone with her/his thoughts, expectations, and immediate choices.

The sense of being an autonomous individual is further strengthened by how computers and other digital technologies reinforce the experience of communication as a process of sending and receiving information. That is, the computer reinforces the conduit view of language (Reddy, 1979) that has played an essential role in maintaining the western view of the individual as the source of rational thought, and the equally powerful and problematic idea that there is such a thing as objective knowledge—that is, knowledge that does not encode the deep and taken-for-granted assumptions of a cultural group. (Bowers, 1995) The sender/receiver (or conduit) model of communication experienced by the student hides a profoundly important though generally ignored characteristic of the language that appears on the screen. While the words and grammatical constructions appear to communicate objective information and data about the real world, these basic building blocks of thought and communication actually encode the metaphorical thought processes of a specific cultural group. (Lakoff, 1987; Johnson 1987; Bowers, 1995, 1997, 2011)

In short, words such as "tradition," "wilderness," "progress," "individualism," "data," and so forth encode and carry forward the earlier metaphorical constructions that underlie modern consciousness. To put it another way, as students adopt the schema of understanding carried forward by these words (such as equating change with a linear form of progress, data as objective, and tradition as impeding modern progress), as well as by other words and images, their thought process is being shaped in a culturally specific way. In short, the computer and other digital technologies mediate the use of language in ways that hide its cultural origins. To reiterate two key points that are often overlooked: print is inherently ethnocentric, and it hides the historical processes of metaphorical thinking that frame the current meaning of the words appearing on the screen.

The experience of self as an autonomous decision maker is further reinforced by the way in which the computer frames how the flow of time is experienced. Unlike many cultures that recognize and value traditions as an integral aspect of the present, and even as having authority that guides present thought and behavior, computers reinforce the modern view of tradition—which places authority in the judgment of the student for deciding whether traditions have any relevance to her/his immediate experience. The subjective, immediate experience of the student sitting in front of the computer or participating in a social network becomes the ultimate source of authority. The unit of time is the immediate problem solving situation, or choice of what is interesting and entertaining. It is a way of experiencing time that makes the relevance of elder knowledge a matter of subjective judgment of the autonomous individual. In effect, the past and future are judged from the perspective of the increasingly rootless individual's immediate interest and experience.

(2) The ability of computers to enable students from different cultures to communicate with each other represents in many instances a positive educational experience. But this gain also involves the reinforcement of a different set of cultural expectations. In addition to substituting communication that is abstract and reductionist for the contextualized face-to-face and intergenerational learning essential to life in orally-based communities, the computer also reinforces a cultural pattern that has become grossly exaggerated by the Industrial Revolution.

All cultures have engaged in the exchange of goods, knowledge, and skills. The means of exchange was largely a barter system, and (in many instances) the weekly market day. The Industrial Revolution, with its need to continually find new markets for the steady stream of technological innovations, has distorted this traditional balance between market and non-market oriented activities that characterized the rhythms of community life. (Berthoud, 1992, p. 75) This drive to turn every aspect of human relationships, knowledge, skill, entertainment, and even the biological basis of life itself into a commodity that can be mass produced and sold on a global scale is now furthered by computers. Unlike the face-to-face interactions of community life, computers involve commodifying the most basic aspect of community—the ability to communicate and to learn from others. The commodification of thought and communication begins with the purchase of a computer, Internet services, and the continual upgrades required by the latest innovations of the computer industry. The commodification process is carried even further by the ability of computers to monitor human activity, which yields data that is being sold to corporations whose goal is to identify potential consumers.

The use of computers in reservation and Third World classrooms may challenge students and sustain their interest in ways that cannot be reproduced in the often lifeless and abstract content of textbooks. However, in becoming dependent upon computers as a means of communication, entertainment, and problem solving, students are drawn into a complex set of cultural patterns and values governed by the forces of the market place. In effect, as students communicate on-line, access information for their reports, and learn the mechanical functions that will enable them to perform in a computer-dependent workplace, they are also being initiated into the seductive consumer lifestyle of continual technological innovation required by the digital phase of the Industrial Revolution. This fact is clearly understood by computer manufacturers such as Apple. Corporate strategists know that there is a connection between the type of computer students first learn to use and their future product loyalty—which is one of the primary reasons they donate computers to schools.

(3) The classroom use of computers also reinforces a key claim of the scientific mode of thinking—that is, the objective nature of knowledge. From the students' perspective, the data, information, images, and graphs appear on the computer screen as objective and accurate representations of some aspect of the real world. Educators currently (and mistakenly) view this capacity of the computer as providing students with the means of constructing their <u>own</u> way of understanding. This capacity to construct, in turn, is seen as the source of new ideas that will lead to even more technological progress. There is also another process of cultural reinforcement that accompanies learning to view relationships and attributes as objectively real.

Unlike the knowledge of nature passed on from generation to generation through mentoring and stories that foreground the culture's sense of moral reciprocity and interdependence, the scientific way of understanding represents the individual as an objective observer in a world where moral values are seen as the expression of pre-scientific ways of understanding. That is, science is supposedly free of cultural bias, including being free of any cultural group's moral tradition of understanding human/nature relationships. While the dominant tradition in science (including computer science) represents the individual as a cultural-free objective observer, the findings of several branches of science are being used to construct a powerful narrative of the creation and evolution of life on this planet. This story of evolution, which increasingly locates the life forming and renewing process in how genes reproduce themselves, is displacing traditional stories of creation that serve as the basis of moral values with an approach that is secular, competitive, and dependent upon the judgment of scientific experts. According to E. O. Wilson, the basic unit in the process of evolution (which operates in an environment of chance and necessity) is the gene. The gene's sole purpose is to replicate itself in future generations, while the environment selects the fittest genes—that is, the better adapted. In *Consilience: The Unity of Knowledge* (1998), Wilson describes the gene in the following way:

> They feel nothing, care for nothing, intend nothing. Their role is simply to trigger the sequence of chemical reactions within the highly structured fertilized cell that orchestrate epigenesis. Their writ extends to the levels of molecule, cell, and organ. This early state of epigenesis, consisting of a series of sequential physicochemical reactions, culminates in the self-assembly of the sensory system and brain....Across evolutionary time, the aggregate choices of many brains determines the Darwinian fate of everything human—the genes, the epigenetic rules, the communicating minds and the culture. (p. 165)

The story of evolution, in locating moral values in the drive of the "selfish gene" to continually replicate itself in future generations, revives the "survival of the fittest" arguments that were influential among western thinkers in the late nineteenth century. Today, a number of scientists are attempting to explain how computers represent the latest stage in this evolutionary process—which they view as part of Nature's process of evolving a global form of super intelligence. Hans Moravec has even argued that computers represent the emergence of the "post biological" phase of the evolutionary process. (1988, p. 5)

In effect, the form of cultural experience reinforced when students use a computer (the sense of autonomy, view of language as a conduit, de-contextualized information, subjective judgment about whether the distant past and future are relevant, commodification of thought and communication, secular-human centered view of nature, and so forth) are being viewed by computer advocates as evidence that computers are helping humans evolve to this next stage of super intelligence. Kevin Kelly, the former editor of *Wired*, concludes his book, *Out of Control: The Rise of Neo-Biological Civilization* (1994) with the statement that the evolutionary process governing the development of computers is "out of our control." That is, the evolutionary process, where only the fittest form of cultural intelligence not only survives but displaces on a global scale other forms of cultural intelligence, is not something that can be resisted. The title of Gregory Stock's book, *Metaman: The Merging of Humans and Machines into a Global Superorganism* (1993), sums up where we are heading, with a professor of developmental biology who teaches at one of the country's premier universities claiming that Stock's "book created in me an optimism, almost a longing for the future."

Unfortunately, the explanations of how computers and other digital technologies are essential to educating students for citizenship and employment in the emerging Information Age ignore that just as the diversity of species is vital to a healthy ecosystem, the maintenance of cultural diversity is equally important. Nor do they take account of the fact that the dominant western pattern of thinking reinforced by computers, while seen by scientists such as E. O. Wilson as more evolutionarily advanced, has an ecological footprint that is undermining the viability of the Earth's ecosystems. That many traditional cultures have taken different pathways of development, and demonstrated the capacity to live in a long-term sustainable relationship with the environment, should be viewed as "better adapted" in an evolutionary sense is also being ignored. When educators claim that the most important question facing resource deprived schools is how to obtain funds to acquire more computers, and to maintain and constantly upgrade them, they are ignoring the deeper questions associated with the culture transforming characteristics of computers. They are also ignoring how science is being used as the basis of a new ideology that justifies the "extinction" of cultures that do not "adapt" to the expanding network of digital-mediated intelligence required by the global economy.

As computers become more integrated into business, government, and the service sectors of the dominant society, the question should not become "How do we shield students from computers?" Rather, it should become "How can we educate students to understand the appropriate and inappropriate uses of these technologies?" This question recognizes that there are always trade-offs, even in what appears to be a constructive use. The latter question is especially important to cultural groups that want to maintain as many of their cultural traditions as possible in the face of modern pressures. As compromises are required in any form of participation in the business/technology and political/ legal sectors of the dominant culture, there are special advantages for students to learn how to use computers. Whether these economic gains exceed the loss of cultural traditions is an open question. What is being suggested here is that, over the long-term, the loss of local knowledge and patterns of moral reciprocity essential to traditional communities will have a dramatic impact on the world's ecological well-being.

The fundamental differences between the form of culture reinforced by the digital revolution and the wide range of cultural ways of knowing that characterize indigenous cultures should be taken into account when considering the special challenges and opportunities that computers pose for teachers. Learning how to use the Internet and other practical applications of computers seems now as essential as learning to read. But there is much more that can be learned from computers if the teacher understands that computers are a cultural-mediating technology; that is, if teachers understand how computers amplify certain cultural ways of knowing while reducing or eliminating others. A strong case can be made that the use of a computer in the classroom provides an opportunity to examine the differences between the dominant culture's way of knowing and value system, with its print-based pattern of thinking, and that of the students' own cultural traditions. Especially important is the ability of the teacher to frame the discussion of cultural differences in terms of the benefits of mutual support networks within a community, as well as in terms of the impact on the viability of natural systems.

The contrast between the modern mind set reinforced by computers and the complex languaging processes involved in the orally based intergenerational experience of community is quite remarkable. How many teachers, for example, engage students in exploring these differences? How many teachers help students understand how the local, richly contextualized rituals, dances, stories, and traditional productive economic activities become distorted and lose their character/identity forming qualities when represented on a computer screen. The passing on of intergenerational knowledge comprises holistic lessons from one generation to the next, incorporating localized environmental knowledge, social skills, and spiritual values—all of which constitutes a major strength of many oral cultures. The lessons engendered in these communal, spiritual, social, and economic activities are not the sort found in schools, computers, or modern lifestyles. They have been the basis of sustainable community and family life, which is often one of the few resources people have left. When these are taken away, as anthropologists have documented everywhere, humanity is diminished.

Hopi *katsina* dances, for example, represent an even better example of what cannot be experienced through a computer. The dances, and the extensive communal preparations for them, provide multi-layered opportunities for a village to come together in a ritual drama, calling on the spirits of the land to bring rain and other blessings. The dances join together young and old men in the *kivas* and women in the *piki* houses—with all coming together in the plaza in ways that pass on the moral and spiritual teachings along with the opportunity to visit and exchange gifts. The opportunity of these reciprocal activities for centering sometimes wavering young people is often lost on the outside observers who do not or cannot appreciate the ecologically and culturally-based frameworks of collective sharing of knowledge and the underlying values they represent.

Instead of turning the computer over to students with vague guidelines for a writing assignment or some other educational task, the teacher needs to be especially aware that the content of educational software provides important opportunities for discussing the cultural non-neutrality of computers. It is an educational opportunity that far exceeds what students will learn from interacting on their own with the thought process encoded in a simulation program. For example, what cultural assumptions are embedded in such popular educational software as SimLife and SimCity? Will students recognize on their own that the assumptions played out in these and other simulation programs are the same assumptions that underlie current effort to globalize a consumer dependent lifestyle that is rapidly overwhelming the life sustaining capacity of the Earth's ecosystems? How does <u>SimCity</u> influence students to think about community? That is, what are represented as the characteristics of a successful and growing community? What are students learning from <u>Storybook Weaver</u>? This is a simulation program that encourages students to write their own stories (rather than listening to the stories told within their communities), and to populate the environment in which their stories are situated with plants and animals that fit their sense of imagination? What are the teacher's responsibilities when the mind of the student (which reflects the patterns of thinking of her/his language community—as well as patterns assimilated from the dominant culture) is meeting the mind of the people who designed the machine and wrote the software? The critical point in this relationship that should be recognized is that these different minds may carry forward different forms of cultural intelligence—and that these differences have important consequences that are not immediately (if ever) understood.

The different educational uses of computers, from participating in electronic communities to learning various forms of decision making and model building, should be seen by teachers as opportunities to help students understand the forms of knowledge and relationships that cannot be communicated through a computer. It would be important to teach why computers cannot communicate the forms of local knowledge passed on through face-to-face relationships. Students should also be encouraged to recognize that computers cannot be used to communicate the following as a living experience: elder knowledge, participation in ceremonies, family relationships and interdependencies, mentoring in clan knowledge and skills, and the stories and practices that carry forward an awareness of how the spirit world requires different expressions of moral reciprocity. In short, the teacher should be able to use the computer as a reference point for clarifying how important aspects of community are transformed or lost when using the computer as the basis of thought, communication, and problem solving. It's not just the cultural amplification and reduction characteristics that need to be discussed, but also why print can only provide a surface knowledge of events and the ecology of ideas and interdependencies.

The teacher should also foster discussions around a different set of questions. It was suggested earlier that computers represent the digital phase of the Industrial Revolution, which continues to have as its primary goal the transformation of more aspects of daily life into commodities that can be mass produced and sold. Teachers should be able to help students understand the different ways in which computers help to bring more aspects of individual, community, and nature itself into the market economy that is undermining traditional forms of communal self-sufficiency. This would also involve examining the different ways in which computers are essential to the process of globalization—a process that has especially important implications for the world's indigenous cultures.

Understanding how computers contribute to turning knowledge, relationships, and even the genetic basis of nature itself into commodities should lead to an examination of the many non-commodified aspects of community life. What are the activities and relationships that are a source of meaning, self-identity, entertainment, mutual support that are not dependent upon some form of consumerism? What are the qualitative differences between having to purchase what meets a need, and possessing the personal skill or engaging in a reciprocal relationship with other members of the community? Another aspect of the spread of a market-oriented culture that needs to be understood is its impact on natural systems.

This is perhaps the most critically important relationship, particularly as it relates to the viability of communities and natural systems. This relationship can be explained in terms of the following circular process: The more people are dependent upon meeting various needs through consumerism, the more they will have to work—which may mean that both parents must work outside the home. The more parents work, the less parenting is done—which too often leads to the parenting being taken over by television and the computer. This, in turn, leads to more exposure to the shaping influence of the advertising industry—which leads to pressure within the family to buy the latest consumer fad. This results in less time and energy for meeting needs in self-sufficient ways. The ecology of consumer dependency leads to more of nature being turned into a resource for the manufacturing process that is eventually cycled back as toxic waste. This part of the cycle, in turn, further undermines the health of natural systems. Increasingly, computers must be seen as an integral part of this destructive cycle of media controlled communication, consumerism, and identity formation.

Whether the uses of computers in Third World classrooms simply subverts the culture's oral traditions, or are used in ways that take account of the genuine cultural gains and losses, depends to a large extent on the teacher's understanding of the cultural transforming characteristics of computers. Again there is a cycle that few experts mention when they urge that computers are the answer to the problems facing schools. Teacher education programs reinforce the idea that computers are a culturally neutral technology ushering us into the Information Age. Courses in other departments of the university communicate the same message. Like so many past relationships between Third World and the Euro-American cultures, the ability of the former to distinguish between the necessary uses of computers and the uses that are destructive of community traditions is being undermined by educational institutions that exert an increasingly powerful influence on the next generation— through the technology that university educated people create and through teachers who too often do not understand the ecologically problematic nature of the modern values and ways of thinking they pass on through the use of computers.

Computer mediated learning not only accelerates the process of alienation from the natural word, it is moving us into a whole new media paradigm—but one that retains the fundamental separations inherent in a Cartesian way of thinking. The danger in this new paradigm, which is based on the most fundamental anti-tradition traditions of modern thinking, is the relegating of diverse ways of knowing to the junk heap of a past that is no longer seen as economically useful. In acculturating Third World students to this new paradigm of commodified knowledge and relationships, which is often hidden under the guise of entertainment, we must ask ourselves if we are, in fact, precluding once and for all their enculturation into the rich environmental knowledge of their own traditions. The educational use of computers, like the Trojan horse that allowed the Greeks to gain access to Troy, needs to be given more careful scrutiny. The losses in the form of assimilation to the environmentally destructive patterns of the Euro-American culture may be far more important than the short-term economic gains and personal conveniences.

References

Basso, Keith. 1996. *Wisdom Sits in Places. Landscape and Language Among the Western Apache.* Albuquerque, NM: University of New Mexico Press.

Berthaud, Gerald. 1992. "Market." In *The Development Dictionary: A Guide to Knowledge as Power,* edited by Wolfgang Sachs. London: Zed Books (70-87).

Bowers, C. A. 1988. *The Cultural Dimensions of Educational Computing: Understanding the Non-Neutrality of Technology.* New York: Teachers College Press.

_____. 1993. *Critical Essays on Education, Modernity, and the Recovery of the Ecological Imperative.* New York: Teachers College Press.

_____. 1995. *Educating for an Ecologically Sustainable Culture: Re-Thinking Moral Education, Creativity, Intelligence, and Other Modern Orthodoxies.* Albany, NY.: State University of New York Press.

_____. 1997. *The Culture of Denial: Why the Environmental Movement Needs a Strategy for Reforming Universities and Public Schools.* Albany, NY.: State University of New York Press.

_____. 2000. *Let Them Eat Data: How Computers Affect Education, Cultural Diversity and the Prospects of Ecological Sustainability.* Athens, GA.: University of Georgia Press.

_____. 2012. *The Way Forward: Educational Reforms that Focus on the Cultural Commons and the Linguistic Roots of the Ecological/Cultural Crises.* Eugene, OR.: The Eco-Justice Press.

Goody, Jack. 1997. *The Domestication of the Savage Mind.* Cambridge, England: Cambridge University Press.

Hale, Constance. "How Do You Say Computer in Hawaiian?" *Wired.* 1995, August (3-10).

Havelock, Eric. 1986. *The Muse Learns to Write: Reflections on Orality and Literacy from Antiquity to the Present.* New Haven CT: Yale University Press.

Heidegger, Martin. 1977. *The Question Concerning Technology and Other Essays.* New York: Harper Colophon Books.

Howe, Craig. 1988. "Cyberspace is no Place for Tribalism." *Wicazo sa Review.* Fall, Vol. 13, No. 2, Fall (19-28).

Ihde, Don. 1979. *Technics and Praxis.* Dortdrecht, Holland: D. Reidel Publishing.

Johnson, Mark. *The Body in the Mind: The Bodily Basis of Meaning, Imagination, and Reason.* 1987. Chicago: University of Chicago Press.

Kelly, Kevin. 1994. *Out of Control: The Rise of Neo-Biological Civilization.* Reading, MA.: Addison-Wesley.

Lakoff, George. 1987. *Women, Fire, and Dangerous Things:What Categories Reveal About the Mind*. Chicago: University of Chicago Press.

Lewis, David. 1995, "Making the Community Connection" *The Computing Teacher*, March (30-32).

Ong, Walter. 1977. *Interfaces of the Word: Studies in the Evolution of Consciousness and Culture*. Ithica, NY: Cornell University Press.

_____. 1982. *Orality and Literacy: The Technologizing of the Word*. London: Methuen.

Reddy, Michael. 1979. "The Conduit Metaphor: A case of Frame Conflict in Our Language About Language." In *Metaphor and Thought*, edited by Andrew Ortony. Cambridge, England: Cambridge University Press.

Rheingold, Howard. 1993. "A Slice of Life in My Virtual Community." In *Global Networks: Computers and International Communication*. Edited by Linda Harasim. Cambridge, MA: MIT Press. (57-80).

Roszak, Theodore. 1994 edition. *The Cult of Information: A Neo Luddite Treatise on High-Tech, Artificial Intelligence, and the True Art of Thinking*. Berkeley: University of California Press.

Sale. Kirkpatrick. 1995. *Rebels Against the Future: The Luddites and Their War on the Industrial Revolution*. Reading, MA: Addison-Wesley.

Stock, Gregory. 1993. *Metaman: The Merging of Humans into a Global Superorganism*. Toronto: Doubleday.

Tannen. Deborah. 1986. "Relative Focus on Involvement in Oral and Written Discourse." In *Literacy, Language, and Learning: The Nature and Consequence of Reading and Writing*, edited by David Olson, Nancy Torrence, and Angela Hildyard. Cambridge, England: Cambridge University Press.

Turkle, Sherry. 1984. *The Second Self: Computers and the Human Spirit*. New York: Simon and Schuster.

_____. 1995. *Life on the Screen: Identity in the Age of the Internet*. New York: Simon and Schuster.

_____. 2011. *Alone Together: Why We Expect More from Technology and Less from Each Other*. New York: Basic Books.

Wilson, E. O. 1998. *Consilience: The Unity of Knowledge*. New York: Alfred A. Knopf.

Winograd, Terry, and Flores, Fernando. 1986. *Understanding Computers and Cognition*. Norwood, NJ.: Ablex Publishing Corp.

Chapter 8

Rethinking Social Justice Issues Within an Eco-Justice Conceptual and Moral Framework

As the social justice issues of class, race, and gender have been the dominant concern of many teacher education and educational studies faculty over the last decades, it is now time to ask whether the recent evidence of global warming, changes in the chemistry of the world's oceans, and the increasing shortage of potable water should lead to developing a new strategy for ameliorating these long standing sources of injustice, homelessness, and poverty. Given the amount of time devoted to discussing class, race, and gender issues with students, as well as the number of books that focus on these issues, little has actually been achieved in effecting the systemic changes required for marginalized social groups to participate on more equal terms in the public arenas of politics, economics, and educational opportunities. Corporations in the United States continue to shape governmental policies that deepen the economic plight of marginalized groups who live at the bottom of the wage scale, while raising the cost of drugs and medical care beyond what they can afford. Overall, the democratic process itself has become degraded by corporate and other special interests to the point where millions of people continue to be mired in poverty and hopelessness.

The recent acceleration of economic globalization, and the deepening of the ecological crises that are now impacting people's daily lives, suggests that a radical rethinking of how to address social justice issues is needed. The growing awareness of these global developments, which includes the lack of moral constraints on the free market system, a weakened labor movement and rapid rise in unemployment, the decline in the size of the middle class, and a need to change the ecological impact on all citizens (even that of the poor who have not been educated about how to live less environmentally destructive lives), means that the old assumptions about achieving a more socially just society need to be re-examined.

Social justice thinking has largely been framed in terms of middle-class assumptions about individualism, progress, a world of unlimited exploitable natural resources, and education as a source of individual empowerment. The ultimate goal of achieving greater social justice for marginalized groups has been to enable them to participate on equal terms in the areas of work, politics, and the culture of consumerism. The guiding priorities of ecojustice-based educational reforms are, on the other hand, both more global in terms of analysis and accountability, and more local in terms of educational strategies that reverse the process of deskilling that is part of the destruction of community systems of mutual support that began with the rise of the techno-scientific based industrial culture. These priorities can be summarized as eliminating environmental racism, resisting the forces that are colonizing Third World cultures and exploiting their natural resources, revitalizing the local cultural and environmental commons that are sites of resistance to the expansion of the industrial/consumer dependent lifestyle, adopting a lifestyle that does not degrade the prospects of future generations, and developing an ecological consciousness that respects the right of natural systems to renew themselves.

Basing daily life on ecojustice criteria means taking account of the impact of the consumer-dependent lifestyle that is being promoted in our public schools and universities by asking whether it is largely responsible for the economic and cultural colonization of Third World societies, as well as the environmental racism that exposes minority groups to the toxic chemicals that the industrial/consumer-oriented culture relies upon. Ecojustice thinking also brings into focus the need to consider the existing community-centered alternatives to the deskilled individual lifestyle that is increasingly dependent upon consumerism— even as the sources of employment become more uncertain because of outsourcing to low-wage regions of the world, and the drive to increase profits by replacing workers with computer-driven machines. As the life-sustaining ecosystems become more degraded, there is also the question of whether the current industrial/consumer-oriented lifestyle that is taken for granted by many educational advocates of social justice is undermining the prospects of future generations. Other concerns of ecojustice thinking include the need to undertake educational reforms that address our responsibility for leaving future generations with sustainable ecosystems, which also means recognizing the right of non-human forms of life to reproduce themselves in sustainable ways.

While the environment is being degraded to the point where the scarcity of protein, water, and energy is driving up prices, thus further impoverishing the already poor, the advertising industry is spending billions of dollars a year in order to perpetuate the public's addiction to consuming the latest fashions, technologies, and forms of entertainment. Public awareness of the environmental changes that scientists are warning about is further obfuscated by the big-box stores and shopping malls that stock their shelves with a super abundance of consumer products—thus further perpetuating the illusion of plenitude. Glitz, easy credit, and continued indifference to the dangers of going deep into debt are just part of the culture that now dominates the majority of the people's lives—that is, those who have not lost their well paying jobs, health and retirement benefits, and are not now reduced to a minimum-wage and near subsistence lifestyle. The poor and marginalized—ranging from single mothers, urban minority youth, migrant farm workers, and a wide range of people whose skin color and lack of educational background disqualify them from other than menial forms of labor in industrial food outlets and other low-paying service-industry jobs, are too focused on meeting the most basic needs of food and shelter to be aware that there are community-centered alternatives to the industrial/consumer lifestyle they have been excluded from participating in. As Barbara Ehrenreich pointed out in an interview with Bill Moyers (2007), the poor live so close to the edge that going without pay for the couple of weeks it takes to find a more high-paying job is unthinkable. In effect, poverty restricts even this most basic option that the middle-class can take for granted. There are now millions of people who are unable to find jobs of any kind, which is a problem that educational reformers have not yet addressed.

The central priorities of ecojustice advocates do not have their roots in abstract theory. Rather, the traditions of intergenerational knowledge and patterns of mutual support that enable people to live in ways where market forces do not dominate everyday life have been around since the beginning of human history. They are still present in every community across North America and in other parts of the world. Historically, these traditions were known as the commons; that is, what is freely shared by the members of the community—which also includes local decision-making. The norms that governed the cultural and environmental commons were passed along orally and differed from culture to culture. The Romans were the first to establish a written record of the commons, which they identified as the local streams, woods, fields, animals, and so forth. The cultural commons, which include the intergenerational knowledge and skills necessary for gathering, preparing, and sharing food, the medicinal properties of plants and where to find them, narratives of courage and of hubris, the rules that governed community members who violated local norms of justice, the sharing of technological skills and craft knowledge, the mythologies and prejudices that regulated who had privileged positions in the community, and so forth, have only recently been identified as part of the commons. The cultural commons also include the voluntary associations that are sources of mutual support within the community, as well as groups that come together to promote agendas that range from providing safe bicycle lanes within the community to supporting the peace efforts of national politicians, and providing aid to people in other parts of the world that have experienced a natural disaster. Unfortunately, the intergenerational sources of empowerment and community self-sufficiency are now being threatened by the market-liberal traditions of private property, anomic individuals who have made a virtue of their cultural amnesia, the expansion of the industrial approach to production and consumption, the growing hegemony of the capitalist ethos, and the rise of corporate power.

While the causes of the economic crisis that is spreading around the world are systemic as well as a function of human greed, it is important to note that the main focus of the media, social-justice politicians, and public is on regaining the jobs that will enable people to return to their previous consumer-dependent lifestyles. That is, there is little discussion of community-centered alternatives that are here being referred to as the cultural commons—and thus little discussion of how the political economy of the local cultural commons can become part of the basis for meeting the daily needs for food, housing, medical care, and education.

If attention were to be given to the lifestyles of people who are more fully engaged in their local cultural commons it would become clearer that they rely less upon a money economy and thus are less exposed to the exploitive forces that are inherent in the industrial governed market place. The voluntary simplicity movement has demonstrated that the political economy of the cultural and environmental commons leads to a different understanding of wealth—one that takes account of skills, mutual support systems, and community well-being. Yet, it is important to recognize that there is still a need for meaningful forms of work that contribute to a living wage. The combination of local decision-making, which is a key feature of many local cultural commons, and the spread of such developments as micro-banks and the pooling of local resources for housing projects and other community infrastructure needs, are also evidence of the need to combine thinking about local self-sufficiency and ecological sustainability.

The relationships between the local cultural commons found in every community today and the industrial/consumer culture have not been mutually supportive. Indeed, the people who promote the expansion of the industrial/consumer-dependent lifestyle, and thus the accumulation of capital, view the largely non-monetized cultural commons as potential markets to be exploited. Their goal is to replace intergenerational skills and patterns of mutual support with new technologies that must be privately owned and with expert systems that represent as sources of backwardness the traditional values and forms of knowledge—such as civil liberties, patterns of returning labor, mentoring, and knowledge of how to live lightly on the land, that have been the strength of many cultural commons. At the time the environmental commons in rural England were being transformed during the early stages of the Industrial Revolution, the process of limiting free access and use on a non-monetized basis, as well as the overturning of local decision-making, was referred to as "enclosure". That is, the enclosure of the environmental commons involved the introduction of private ownership and integration into a money economy, which often led to decision-making being transferred to distant owners—and later to corporations that made increasing profits their primary goal.

Now that we can recognize the cultural beliefs and practices, which now include cyberspace, as part of the cultural commons that enable community members to be less dependent upon a money economy, it is possible to recognize the many ways in which different aspects of the local cultural commons are being enclosed by today's market forces—as well as by ideologies, technologies, prejudices, and silences. Public schools and universities continue to be complicit in reinforcing the cultural assumptions that further undermine the viability of the cultural commons, especially the cultural commons of ethnic groups, even as environmental scientists are working to conserve what remains of the environmental commons. Many social-justice oriented faculty continue to reinforce many of the same cultural assumptions that gave conceptual direction and moral legitimacy to the industrial/consumer-dependent lifestyle even as they criticize the exploitive nature of capitalism. These shared assumptions include the idea of the autonomous individual, the progressive nature of change, an anthropocentric view of human/ nature relationships, and the drive to impose these assumptions on other cultures under the rubric of "development", as well as the same silences about the local community sources of self-sufficiency and mutual support. (Sachs,1992).

While the diversity of the world's cultural commons currently represents sites of resistance to economic globalization, it is important to avoid romanticizing the cultural commons. In many cultures, including the local communities across North America, the cultural commons also include narratives and traditions that perpetuate different forms of discrimination and economic exploitation. That is, the stoning to death of the woman who seeks to marry outside of her tribe, the market-liberal ideology that equates social progress with an economy that makes survival of the fittest the ultimate test of individual success, and the various forms of racial, class, and gender prejudices also have their roots in the traditions of some cultural commons. Ironically, these non-monetized traditional beliefs and practices (which have dire economic and social consequences for those who are the subjects of discrimination) were and still are generally sustained in communities which may also possess networks of mutual support that reduce reliance on consumerism—and that have a smaller ecological footprint.

The local cultural commons should not be regenerated and supported just because they represent alternatives to the industrial/ consumer-oriented culture that is being globalized. Rather, the different traditions of the cultural commons need to be examined in terms of whether they support traditions of civil liberties, as well as moral reciprocity in the treatment of all members of the community as deserving the right to an equal opportunity to develop their personal talents and to make their contributions to regenerating the life-supporting cultural commons. Challenging the traditions of the cultural commons that are sources of exploitation and marginalization should also be part of a more global and ecologically informed ecojustice pedagogy.

As pointed out in *Educational Reforms for the 21st Century: How to Introduce Ecologically Sustainable Reforms in Teacher Education and Curriculum Studies* (2011), the unique characteristics of the cultural and environmental commons require a radically different approach than the current emphasis on making individual emancipation, promoting the students' construction of their own knowledge, and making higher test scores the primary foci of educational reform. There are a number of unique characteristics of the cultural commons that an ecojustice pedagogy needs to take into account. The first is that most of the traditions that members of a community participate in on a daily basis are taken for granted, such as the tradition of English speakers using the subject-verb-object pattern of oral and written communication, assuming they are innocent until proven guilty before a jury of peers, and using language as a conduit in a sender/receiver process of communication—to cite just a few of the taken for granted patterns of daily life. The taken for granted status of most aspects of the local cultural commons is important for several reasons. In being part of tacit, contextual, and largely taken for granted experience, they are mostly excluded from the curriculum of public schools and universities. In being excluded from the curriculum at all levels of the formal education process, and in being largely taken for granted by members of the community who are at the same time being constantly indoctrinated with the message that change is essential to progress, the loss (that is, enclosure) of different traditions of the cultural commons too often go unnoticed. The exceptions are the people who are consciously carrying forward one of the traditions of the cultural commons, such as weaving, protecting civil liberties, utilizing craft knowledge and skill, participating in local theater, and so forth.

The taken for granted nature of the individual's experience of the cultural commons, which may include racist and gender forms of discrimination, is just one of the characteristics of daily experience that require a different approach to teaching and learning than is found in current approaches that are based on many of the same cultural assumptions (or what I have referred to elsewhere as root metaphors) that underlie the industrial/consumer-oriented culture that is overshooting the life-sustaining capacity of natural systems. The emphasis on explicit forms of knowledge, which is reinforced by reliance on print-based knowledge, testing, and supposedly objective knowledge, marginalizes the importance of helping students recognize the differences between their experiences in the cultural commons and in the market/consumer-oriented culture.

Another bias in current approaches to education that can be traced back to Plato's argument that *pure thinking* leads to universal truths that are more reliable than thinking grounded in embodied/culturally-influenced experiences. The western theorists who followed in this tradition of assuming that abstract words are a more accurate source of knowledge also were unaware of the nature and ecological importance of their local cultural commons. Indeed, they held in contempt the forms of face-to-face, intergenerationally shared knowledge and skill, and relegated them to low-status knowledge.

This tradition is still evident in the thinking of current educational reformers who assume that words such as individualism, democracy, tradition (which reproduces the Enlightenment assumptions of being a source of backwardness and special privileges), intelligence, and progress have a universal meaning. (Ayers, Quine, and Stovall, 2009). These educational reformers continue to ignore how the analogs that frame the meaning of these metaphors carry forward the misconceptions of earlier thinkers. This pattern of thinking further marginalizes an awareness of the embodied experiences in the different community traditions that are being referred to here as part of the cultural commons. One of the consequences of the silences about the nature and complexity of the cultural commons, as well as the constant reminder that traditions are impediments to progress, which are being reinforced in most areas of the public school and university curriculum, is that students enter adulthood without an awareness of the different economic and ideological forces that are enclosing what remains of the cultural commons. For most of them, the industrial/consumer culture is the arena in which they will personally succeed or fail—and the outcome of their individual quests remain disconnected in their thinking from the rapid rate of degradation of the world's ecosystems.

There is now a major body of writing that addresses both the various ways in which public schools reproduce the culture's traditions of class and other forms of discrimination, as well as the reforms that need to be undertaken in order to achieve a more equitable society. Criticism of prejudicial language, silences in the curriculum, preconceptions about the potential (or lack thereof) of already marginalized students, tracking and other systemic forms of discrimination, have been the mainstays of educational foundations and educational studies courses for the past several decades. While there have been some social justice gains, particularly in the areas of race and gender, there remains much to be done—especially since the changes resulting from economic globalization and global warming will have the greatest impact on minority groups whose economic gains have been, at best, both minimal and fragile. Critiques of the beliefs and values that have kept people of color, women, and other people restricted by other class barriers have actually been critiques of the reactionary traditions found within some cultural commons. Unfortunately, the theories that framed these critiques were not informed about the complex nature of the cultural commons. The main consequence of this lack of understanding is that the aspects of the cultural commons that hold out the prospect of finding community-centered alternatives to the negative impact of the industrial culture have not been part of the well-intended efforts to use the schools to eliminate the sources of poverty and injustice.

The use of a sociological interpretative framework seemed ideally suited to bringing into focus economic, political, and educational inequities. Unfortunately, it has led to ignoring the questions that would have arisen if a more anthropologically informed interpretative framework had been relied upon. Awareness of a deep understanding of cultural differences could easily have brought into question how notions of individual freedom and equality could be reconciled with the importance that has been given in recent years to avoiding cultural colonization. For example, the western ideal of individual freedom and the diversity of non-western cultures do not easily fit together. Another limitation of the sociological interpretative framework is that it keeps the analysis and recommendations for reform on human-to-human relationships, with the human-to-nature relationships being ignored. The evidence for this claim can easily be substantiated by reading educational writers who have most influenced how the analysis of class, race, and gender has been framed—especially writers such as Samuel Bowles, Herb Gintis, Michael Apple, Henry Giroux, and Peter McLaren. Recently, however, Bowles and Gintis have been writing about the importance of the commons, and McLaren has now turned attention to explaining how Marxism can guide educational reforms that address issues of sustainability. (McLaren, 2005) The key point is that today's educational discourse on class, race, and gender continues to ignore, with only a few exceptions, the implications of the ecological crises for the very social groups they want to emancipate.

The use of the cultural commons as the conceptual framework for analyzing the various forms of discrimination, as well as for guiding educational reforms, has several advantages that a sociological framework lacks. To reiterate: the cultural commons represent all of the forms of knowledge, values, practices, and relationships that have been handed down over generations that have been the basis of individual and community self-sufficiency—and that have enabled members of the community to be less dependent upon a money economy now undergoing systemic changes. While the previous discussion of the reactionary and, in some cases, horrific practices of some of the world's cultural commons need to be kept in mind, there are other characteristics of self-sufficiency that existed prior to what Karl Polanyi called the *Great Transformation*, when the emergence of the industrial system of production led to the enclosure of the environmental commons. (Polanyi, 2002) Kirkpatrick Sale summed up in *Rebels Against the Future: The Luddites and Their War on the Industrial Revolution* how the survival and global expansion of the industrial system of production and consumption depended upon the enclosure of the cultural commons. (1995) As he put it,

> All that "community" implies—self-sufficiency, mutual aid, morality in the market place, stubborn tradition, regulation by custom, organic knowledge instead of mechanistic science—had to be steadily and systematically disrupted and displaced. All the practices that kept the individual from being a consumer had to be done away with so that the cogs and wheels of an unfettered machine called the 'economy' could operate without interference, influenced merely by invisible hands and inevitable balances" p. 38.

Sale does not refer to the community traditions of self-sufficiency as the cultural commons, but he accurately makes the point that the industrial/consumer-dependent culture requires the destruction of the different forms of intergenerational knowledge, skills and mutually supportive relationships that enabled people to live less consumer-dependent lives. In effect, he is describing how the success of the industrial system of production and consumption required the destruction of the local cultural and environmental commons. What is ironic is that the kind of individual required by the industrial/consumer-dependent culture is the autonomous individual being promoted by many of today's educational reformers. It is also important to note that the lack of intergenerational knowledge that reduces dependence upon consumerism contributes to an important aspect of poverty that is seldom discussed—even though it leads to the forms of poverty that threaten the individual's health and leads to other forms of insecurity.

Unlike the limited conceptual possibilities of a sociological interpretative framework and vocabulary, the cultural commons is the phrase that encompasses the traditions of community that are nested in larger social and ecological systems. These traditions, as mentioned earlier, range from local approaches to growing and preparing food (as alternatives to an industrialized system) that is so damaging to ecosystems and to intergenerational approaches to healing that differ from the highly monetized and industrial approaches of today's medicine (which are increasingly becoming dependent upon patenting indigenous knowledge of the medicinal properties of plants). (Shiva, 1996) Depending upon the local community and cultural traditions, the intergenerational knowledge also includes the creative arts passed on through mentoring that differ from the star system of commercialized music and visual arts; and as well as narratives of the labor, feminist, and civil rights movements rather than the mind-numbing television sit-coms that also serve to hook viewers to the multi-billion advertising industry. The traditions of civil rights that go back to the Magna Carta of 1215 are also part of the cultural commons.

Unfortunately, they are now being enclosed by the growing alliance between market-liberal-dominated governments, corporations, universities, and the military establishment. A more fine-grained analysis of the differences between the cultural commons and the industrial/consumer-dependent culture that is now being globalized would involve a discussion of the differences between community mentors and university-trained experts who have an ego and economic investment in imposing abstract theory-based solutions on people's lives, between face-to-face and computer-mediated communication, between community traditions of reciprocity where work is returned and work that has to be paid for, between developing personal interests and skills and being a consumer of other people's talents, as well as between the embodied experiences of being in the natural environment and the disembodied experience of sitting in front of a computer screen with its often violent simulation games that deaden the capacity for empathy and moral responsibility.

There are two other characteristics of the cultural commons that have special significance. The first is that they exist in every community and can be fully recognized only by an in-depth description of the cultural patterns that unconsciously influence the experience of preparing and sharing a meal, playing a game, telling a story, writing poetry, marching in an anti-war demonstration, protesting experimentations and other forms of animal exploitation, working with others in renewing habitats, and so forth. The cultural commons are largely taken for granted and thus unrecognized aspects of daily life—and can best be brought to attention through actual participation and ethnographic/phenomenological descriptions rather than through abstract theory and print-based descriptions. The second characteristic that needs to be reiterated, especially in light of the rate of global warming, is that what the industrial culture had to destroy, as Sale put it, are the intergenerational traditions that have smaller adverse impacts on the ecological systems.

Most aspects of the cultural commons in western countries rely to some degree on what has to be purchased. However, even this small degree of dependence makes a great deal of difference in terms of meeting the criteria of eco-justice. By being more intergenerationally connected, a revitalized cultural commons *reduces* the need for a system of production that has to dispose of vast amounts of toxic wastes (usually in the neighborhoods of the poor and marginalized). It also reduces the need to exploit the resources of Third World cultures and to integrate them into a global market system. As these cultures are able to regenerate their own cultural commons they are able to resist more effectively the West's efforts to colonize them in the name of development, democracy, and modernization—god-words that are based on western assumptions about individualism, progress, and the messianic drive to impose a consumer-dependent lifestyle on other cultures. The lifestyle that is more oriented toward cultural commons skills and activities of mutual support, and less on consumerism that degrades the environment and thus the prospects of future generations, meets yet another concern of eco-justice advocates. In possessing the skills and participating in the community systems of mutual support, the individual is more likely to resist the market-oriented ideology that equates the exploitation of species and habitats with progress. This characteristic of the cultural commons meets the last criteria of recognizing that natural systems have a right to reproduce themselves as part of the layered nesting of interdependent ecosystems—and not to be reduced to an economic resource.

This list of the ecologically sustainable and morally coherent characteristics of the cultural commons brings out what is missing in most of the educational discourse on how to eliminate discrimination in the areas of class, race, and gender. It also brings into focus the viable alternatives for addressing the estimated one billion lives that exist on one dollar a day, and are mired in the culture of poverty marked by a lack of food security and adequate housing. As global warming accelerates in the next few decades, as the world's oceans become less reliable sources of protein, and as droughts and severe weather systems contribute to mass migrations of people, the lives of the poor will become even more desperate as they expand in number. The double bind of relying upon sources of energy to keep the industrial system expanding (thus accelerating the rate of global warming) will intensify the willingness of corporations to outsource production facilities not only to low-wage regions but also to regions that still have easily accessed sources of energy. As the ecological crisis deepens, and the seemingly unrelenting drive to continue expanding profits in an increasingly stressed world becomes more difficult, it will be the people who continue to occupy the bottom rung of the economic/political/educational hierarchy who will continue to suffer the most.

The irony is that the ancient pathway of human development that still exists in rural and urban communities, and that represents an essential part of a post-industrial alternative, continues to be ignored—even by the few educational theorists who are beginning to recognize the ecological crisis. What now has to be avoided is the endless repetition that there is an ecological crisis and that capitalism is primarily responsible. Thoughtful people already understand the connections between these two phenomena. Instead, advocates of social justice need to explore the pedagogical and curricular implications of how to introduce students, including the already marginalized students, to the life-enhancing possibilities that exist in the cultural commons of their local communities—and that are part of the cultural commons of the dominant culture that protects the rights of various minority cultures. There is a direct connection between the enclosure of the traditions of civil liberties that are the basis of democracy and the growing dominance of corporations, market liberal politicians, religious fundamentalists, and the military establishment that views its mission as protecting the global interests of market liberals. There is also a connection in America between the number of marginalized groups who suffer the most deaths and catastrophic injuries from military actions that result from the logic of economic globalization. Knowledge of how to protest against the various forms of economic and political oppression is also part of the cultural commons—which includes the narratives of past protest movements, strategies that have proved most successful, and even the protest songs and iconography associated with past peace movements. The current drive to install total surveillance systems of a country's citizens as a defense against terrorism further undermines their civil liberties, and will be used by police to identify the leaders of movements protesting various forms of social injustice—including environmental activists.

Pedagogical and Curricular Implications

The future prospects of the poor and marginalized are inextricably tied to the future prospects of the cultural and environmental commons. With the outsourcing of work, computer-driven automation that reduces the need for workers, and downsizing in order to improve corporate profits, the prospects of upward mobility that have been an expectation of past generations, though unevenly realized, are being rapidly diminished. Given this reality, placing greater emphasis on educational reforms that help to regenerate the cultural commons should not be interpreted as meaning that all students, regardless of social class and ethnic background, should not acquire the knowledge that will enable them to find meaningful work that supports a basic standard of living. Just as most aspects of the cultural commons require some degree of dependence upon the industrial system of production and consumption, public schools and universities need to ensure that the students at the bottom of economic and social pyramid have the opportunity to learn what is required for careers and employment that are non-exploitive. At the same time, changes need to be introduced at all levels of the educational system that will enable students to learn about the community-centered alternatives that contribute to the transition to a post-industrial future—namely, the cultural commons. In discussing the unique characteristics of a pedagogy and curriculum that introduce students to the ecological and community-sustaining importance of the cultural commons, it is important to keep in mind that we are in a transition phase of cultural development. Thus, the following discussion of pedagogical and curriculum reforms must also be viewed in this light.

If we consider the basic tension between the industrial/ consumer-oriented culture and the characteristics of the cultural commons that strengthen mutual support, develop skills and personal talents, and ensure moral reciprocity among all members of the community, it becomes clear what the role of the classroom teacher/professor should be. Instead of promoting the high-status forms of knowledge and values that contribute to the further expansion of the industrial/consumer-oriented culture, the role of the classroom teacher and university professor should be that of a mediator who helps students become aware of the fundamental differences between participation in the cultural commons and the culture of industrial production and consumption. Being a mediator requires an understanding of what students are most likely to take for granted as they move daily between participation in the two sub-cultures. The pedagogical task is to encourage students to name what would otherwise be taken for granted. Naming taken-for-granted patterns of thinking and behavior, as we learned from both the feminist and civil rights movements, is the first step to making them explicit, which is essential for developing communicative competence. Like the mediator in labor disputes, the teacher's mediator role precludes giving students the answers about which aspects of the cultural commons and the industrial/consumer-oriented culture need to be rejected or renewed. The techno-scientific basis of the industrial culture has made many important contributions to improving the quality of human life, and now has the potential to help reduce our carbon footprint. Thus, the task of being a mediator should not be reduced to that of an ideologue who has pre-conceived answers, and who enforces the silence about what her/his ideology cannot explain. Similarly, ideology should not guide how the students are to think about their embodied experiences within the cultural and environmental commons.

The initial step in teaching and learning that fits the model of a mediator is to encourage students to describe their embodied/ culturally-influenced experiences as they move between the two sub-cultures. There are specific questions that students need to be reminded to ask: Does the experience in a cultural commons activity contribute to the development of personal skills and the discovery of talents? Does it contribute to a sense of community self-sufficiency and mutual support? Does it require exploiting others who are less advantaged? What is its impact on natural systems? Does it contribute to an awareness of what needs to be intergenerationally renewed and of the need to be able to mentor others? Does it lead to different forms of empowerment, such as the ability to exercise communicative competence in resisting further forms of enclosure of skills and patterns of mutual support that result in an increased dependency upon a money economy? What is its ecological footprint? These same questions need to be explored by students as they participate in various aspects of the industrial/consumer-oriented culture.

In examining the differences in experience between preparing and sharing a meal with others and eating in a fast food outlet; between face-to-face communication and reading; between gardening and being dependent upon industrially prepared food; between participating in one of the creative arts and being a consumer of commercially promoted artistic performances; between developing skills associated with a craft that extends one's talents and purchasing what has been industrially produced (increasingly in a low-wage region of the world); the differences in personal development will quickly become apparent. And this awareness of differences, if framed in light of the ecological crisis and the changes resulting from economic globalization, is essential to the recovery of local democracy that has been one of the hallmarks of the diverse cultural commons that have not been based on ideologies and mythologies that have privileged the few over the many.

Another responsibility of the teacher/professor's mediating role is to ensure that students become aware of the narratives that provide an account of various social-justice movements—starting with the earliest beginnings of the traditions of civil liberties in the West. These include habeas corpus, the right to a fair trial by a jury of peers, separation of powers, and an independent judiciary. The narratives that provide an understanding of the labor movements that struggled to achieve safe working conditions, a living wage, and the right of workers to organize politically, should also be part of the curriculum. The feminist as well as the civil rights movements also should be part of a commons-oriented curriculum. Again the tensions between the cultural commons and the industrial/consumer-oriented culture that are now being globalized, and that are major contributors to the ecological crisis, will inevitably come out—and be a major focus of class discussions.

The ecological crisis, as well as the increasing number of the world's population that is moving from a subsistence existence into one of dire poverty, make it particularly important that the teacher/professor introduce students to the history of different ways in which the cultural commons are being enclosed. The following questions will bring into focus different forms of enclosure: How did the western philosophers' reliance on unacknowledged culturally-influenced interpretative frameworks (which can also be understood as root metaphors that frame the historically layered process of analogic thinking) contribute to the enclosure of the cultural commons? How has the rise of western science contributed to the enclosure of local knowledge of healing, agricultural practices, reliance on local materials, and so forth? What role have various religions played in strengthening the cultural commons and, on the other hand, in representing the exploitation of the commons by market forces as carrying out God's plan for those who are to be saved? What were the intellectual influences that marginalized the importance of the workers' skills, their control of the tempo of work and use of technologies? What are the current techno-scientific and market forces that are threatening the genetic diversity of seeds, and local knowledge of how to adapt agricultural practices to the characteristics of local soils and weather patterns?

In addition to introducing, particularly as the students move into the upper grades and onto the university, the various histories of different forms of enclosure, the role of being a mediator also requires that students be introduced to how different cultures have sustained their cultural and environmental commons while at the same time ensuring that their local markets did not dominate the patterns and values of everyday life (W. Sachs, 1992; W. Sachs, 1993). Knowledge of the intergenerational traditions of other cultural approaches to the cultural and environmental commons will enable students to gain a better perspective on whether the current myth that equates the western scientific-technological and market-driven approaches to creating greater dependence on what is industrially produced and consumed should be the basis of development in other cultures. There is a need to enable a large percentage of the world's population that is mired in poverty to obtain a decent standard of living and to enable them to experience more than a life of drudgery and stunted development. The critical question is whether the further enclosure of the diversity of the world's cultural commons will achieve this end.

To this point, the discussion of the teacher/professor's role as a mediator between the students' culturally embedded experiences in the local cultural commons and in the workplace and shopping malls of the industrial culture has been general in nature. It is now necessary to address how to engage students from a variety of backgrounds that make them especially vulnerable to the prejudices currently perpetuated by the educational system's emphasis on the high-status knowledge that perpetuates poverty and deepens the ecological crisis. As mentioned earlier, every culture has its own intergenerational traditions of preferred foods, approaches to the creative arts, healing practices, ways of understanding moral reciprocity, craft knowledge, narratives of past achievements and leaders, mentors in various arts and crafts, understanding of social justice, and so forth. For example, in the largely Hispanic community in San Francisco one will find that many of the walls of buildings that previously were used to advertise cigarettes and liquor have been reclaimed as part of the cultural commons. Giant murals now depict past struggles, important cultural leaders, and visions of what the future should hold for Hispanic communities.

The same reclaiming of this part of the cultural commons can be found in Detroit and other major cities. Other examples of the cultural commons can be seen in the community gardens where traditional foods are grown, in the local poets, artists, writers, and musicians who are willing mentors of the community's youth. There are elders and people who take responsibility for keeping alive the oral history of the group, just as there are living traditions of how assist the especially vulnerable to the problems of extreme poverty, old age, and hopelessness. The nature of these cultural commons varies from community to community, from ethnic group to ethnic group. As the cultural commons of these ethnic and marginalized groups are nested in the cultural commons of the larger society, with its traditions of civil liberties, of achieving legal redress of discriminatory practices, and of effecting changes through an admittedly flawed democratic process, it is important that these traditions also be recognized as essential aspects of what marginalized students should claim as their cultural commons.

The starting point in a commons-oriented curriculum is to have students conduct a survey of their local cultural commons, as well as the aspects of the larger cultural commons that they have a right (in spite of past exclusions) to participate in. The survey should involve learning who the elders and mentors are, who the keepers of the community memory are, what forms of cultural commons activities exist—such as playing chess, painting, writing poetry, musical performances, gardening, working with wood and metal, volunteerism, and political action groups. In a word, the survey should cover the activities and relationships within the community that are less reliant upon a money economy—and that lead to the development of skills and interests that contribute to a less damaging ecological footprint.

After the survey has been undertaken, the process of learning to make explicit the differences between their culturally nested experiences with different activities within the cultural commons and in the world of industrial work and consumerism can begin. This process of learning to recognize differences that otherwise are taken for granted as the students move between the two sub-cultures, and to name them, provides the linguistic and conceptual basis for the communicative competence necessary for resisting further forms of enclosure by market and scientific/technological forces. Resistance may take the form of overcoming the silences about the nature and importance of the local cultural commons being perpetuated in public schools and universities. It also may take the form of resisting the false promises of developers who want to attract the large commercial enterprises that will eliminate the small shop keepers and service providers, as well as the open physical spaces that enable members of the community to connect with the natural world, to have community gardens and places for children and others to play, and to escape the pressures of the media and the temptations of the shopping malls. Communicative competence is also necessary to giving voice to what aspects of the techno-scientific/industrial culture need to be abandoned as ecologically unsustainable—and which aspects can make a contribution to improving the lives of people while still having a smaller ecological footprint.

One of the failures of the educational theorists who have been writing about the need for educational reforms that address the seemingly intractable problems of class, race, and gender discrimination is that they have continued to use the metaphors of *individualism, progress, emancipation, intelligence, tradition,* and so forth, that carry forward the analogs formed in the distant past by theorists who ignored cultural differences, the nature and importance of the cultural and environmental commons, and the existence of ecological limits. In effect, the arguments for addressing the issues of race, class, and gender have been based on a metaphorical language that has been frozen over time, and that continues to put out of focus the intergenerational relationships and knowledge that provide alternatives to the form of individualism that is dependent upon consumerism to meet daily needs. Reliance upon the metaphorical language that gave conceptual legitimacy to the rise and current globalization of an industrial/consumer dependent lifestyle can also be understood as yet another unrecognized example of how language continues to colonize the present by past ways of understanding

Learning to participate in what remains of the local cultural commons, and in developing new skills and non-monetized relationships will have the effect of expanding how intelligence is understood— from that of an individual attribute that is subjectively centered to understanding that intelligence is communal, intergenerational, and enhanced through participation with others, and with the environment. As the communal and intergenerational nature of intelligence may be the source of prejudices and environmentally destructive lifestyles, it is important that teachers/professors help students recognize the forms of intelligence that are destructive of human possibilities, as well as the ways of thinking that are informed by today's understanding of social and ecojustice. This has been part of the curriculum that addresses various forms of discriminatory relationships and patterns of thinking. Too often this emphasis on emancipation has reinforced the idea that critical thinking is the expression of individual autonomy. Making the students' culturally-influenced experiences in the local cultural and environmental commons an integral part of the curriculum will help reconstitute how individualism should be understood—from that of being autonomous and essentially alone to recognizing that one of the unique characteristics of life is being in an ecology of relationships that constantly lead to a redefinition of self that reflects changes in the social and environmental context. The word "tradition," which still carries forward the reductionist thinking of Enlightenment writers, will also cease to be an abstraction that misrepresents the complexity of daily experience in both the cultural commons and in the industrial/consumer-oriented culture. Instead of thinking that change is always a progressive force, the students' reflections on their experiences within both sub-cultures will lead to a more complex and critically informed understanding of which traditions need to be carried forward and renewed, and which traditions need to be rejected as environmentally destructive and as sources of injustice.

One of the metaphors that is in special need of being associated with new analogs is *environment,* which is now understood either as the background within which human experience takes place or as an exploitable resource. If the teacher/professor explains, and has students test out in terms of their own embodied experiences, how different environments can be understood as ecologies—and that ecologies include both the interactions and interdependencies within natural systems as well as within cultures (and the interdependencies between culture and nature) students are more likely to be aware of the different ways in which their activities impact the sustainable characteristics of natural systems. Students still rooted in the beliefs of their indigenous heritage already possess this awareness, but students who have been uprooted from their cultural traditions, which may not have been ecologically-centered in the first place, will need to develop this awareness. And this awareness will be essential to slowing the rate of environmental degradation that will impact them the hardest in coming years.

The challenge now is for the proponents of educational reforms that address the issues of class, race, and gender to recognize that an approach to achieving social justice for the millions of marginalized students cannot be based on the same deep cultural assumptions that created the industrial/consumer-oriented culture that is largely responsible for the injustices that continue to stunt the potential of students. This challenge will be particularly difficult to address as few of today's proponents of educational reform have given attention to how language helps to organize their own patterns of thinking in ways that reproduce the silences and cultural assumptions of past theorists who contributed to today's double bind patterns of thinking. The problem is that the double bind thinking of these self-proclaimed social justice theorists continues to equate progress with achieving greater equality of opportunity for marginalized groups to live a middle class consumer dependent lifestyle—while the world is moving closer to the ecological tipping point scientists are warning about.

References

Ayers, William, Theresa Quine, and David Stovall (editors). (2009) *Handbook of Socal Justice in Education.* New York: Routledge.

Bowers, C. A. (2011). *Educational Reforms for the 21st Century: How to Introduce Ecologically Sustainable Reforms in Teacher Education and Curriculum Studies.* Eugene, OR. The Eco-Justice Press.

Moyers, B. (2007) Bill Moyer's journal, August 3, 2007. Available at www.pbs.org/moyers/journal/08032007/transcripts1.html.

Polanyi, Karl. (2001 edition) *The Great Transformation.* Boston: Beacon Press.

Sachs, Wolfgang. (editor) (1992) *The Development Dictionary: A Guide to Knowledge as Power.* London: Zed Books.

_____. (editor, 1993) *Global Ecology: The New Arena of Political Conflict.* London: Zed Books.

Sale, Kirkpatrick. (1995) *Rebels Against The Future: The Luddites and Their War on the Industrial Revolution.* Reading, MA.: Addison-Wesley.

Shiva, Vandana (1996) *Protecting Our Biological and Intellectual Heritage in the Age of Biopiracy.* New Delhi: Research Foundation for Science, Technology and Natural Resource Policy.

www.ingramcontent.com/pod-product-compliance
Lightning Source LLC
Chambersburg PA
CBHW070857050426
42334CB00053B/1833